Proper Puddings

In memory of my father, John Alan Maurice Evans, 1936-2009, who liked puddings.

Proper Puddings

by

Hugh Evans

RUNCIBLE BOOKS

Designed by Jonny Hughes
Edited by Jo Swinnerton

This edition first published in Great Britain in 2012 by Runcible Books.

A CIP record for this book is available from the British Library.

ISBN 978-0-9574925-0-9

Printed and bound in Great Britain by CPI Antony Rowe, Chippenham

Contents

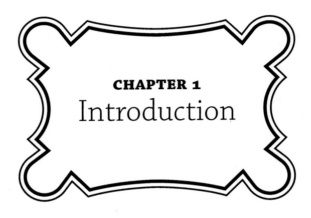

CHAPTER 1

Introduction

I AM SURE that I am not alone in looking at the end of a menu first. Pudding is rightly conceived to be the crowning glory of a meal. I have noticed that anyone who comes to dinner, even if they claim to have no interest in pudding, will normally have two helpings and then talk about it afterwards to the exclusion of all other matters culinary. I suppose this is because puddings are so wonderful, and they come last and are therefore the most memorable part of a meal. But part of the reason is that they are somewhat rarer than they should be. People seldom show much reaction to the main course because, after all, that is what dinner necessarily includes, but a proper pudding is a little unusual. The last course is more likely these days to be a 'dessert', about which more later.

I have been cooking and eating puddings, and reading recipes and cookery books on puddings, for many, many years. But I have never found a book on puddings that has met my particular needs. The recipes are often unnecessarily complicated; none explores properly the many interesting variations of each type of pudding that can be made; and many are written by cooks who seem to have no real passion for puddings. So, in this Work I will attempt to Remedy these Defects and produce a book for people who, like me, love puddings and want to cook them more often with a minimum of fuss.

What is a pudding?

I wouldn't want to be too prescriptive about the precise definition of pudding. There is a perfectly proper use of 'pudding' in, for instance 'Yorkshire pudding', which is clearly not sweet. However, what I mean by pudding is a dish that is (1) hot, (2) sweet, and (3) solid and substantial, if not stodgy. The latter is of vital importance. Puddings are, or should be, rich, unctuous, filling, comforting; an almost sufficient justification for winter, along with a good fish pie or the Six Nations rugby tournament. If the eyes are the window of the soul, puddings are its hot-water bottle.

To narrow the field further, puddings are almost invariably simple to make, require no great accuracy or finesse in measuring, mixing or cooking, take quite a time to cook and are normally best with custard. In this way, puddings are quite different from 'sweets' or 'desserts', which tend to have none of the above characteristics, save for being sweet. However, I have included in this book some puddings of this kind, which are not, by my definition, proper puddings at all. But I try not to be dogmatic about these things. Many people do like them, they are good in the summer, and I sometimes make them in the winter, too, as a supplement to a proper pudding if several people are coming round to supper.

While proper puddings have seen something of a renaissance in the last few years, there is a general prejudice against them on the grounds that they are fattening and unhealthy. There is, of course, some truth in this. But lower-calorie foods are simply not as tasty. The solution, I think, is twofold. First, don't eat puddings every day; but I know no one who does, not even me. Secondly, take some exercise. I cycle home from work before making puddings.

Puddings are simple

As a man, I don't have the patience for complicated puddings, so there are very few in this book that would take more than half an hour's preparation, and most will take much less. Furthermore, very few puddings take any real skill to make, which is a blessing because I haven't got much. The only partial exceptions are in the Improper Puddings chapter at the end. Soufflés, in particular, need a bit of practice. I suppose to a lesser extent pies and tarts all require some modest amount of skill, but it can be acquired fairly easily.

Having said that, I will admit that puddings often take quite a long time to actually cook, once assembled. While you will be able to make a crumble or bread pudding during the week to eat that evening, a proper steamed pudding is normally a weekend affair, as it takes a couple of hours to steam. However, don't let this put you off – while they are in or on the stove, most puddings take care of themselves, so they are not time-consuming.

How this book works

I thought that a chapter on ingredients, weights and measures and other technical stuff might help the beginner, who I am keen to encourage. Then I move on to how to make custard. This is the *fons et origo* of most good puddings. From there, I progress through types of pudding in roughly ascending order of difficulty, from the ridiculously simple to the moderately straightforward.

The next three chapters have the easiest and probably most common and popular puddings. Milk puddings are unbelievably easy to make and take no time to assemble. Crumbles and bread and butter puddings can be made, in my experience, by an intelligent five-year-old.

There follow chapters on boiled, steamed and baked puddings, which are the heart of this book. The essential ingredients are suet or butter and flour or breadcrumbs. (Suet puddings are the favourite of all lawyers.) I then turn to tarts and pies. They do require some technique, which is well worth acquiring by means of a little practice. After a chapter on assorted other proper puddings,

I then, somewhat reluctantly, describe how to make a few light and improper puddings.

As part of my crusade to encourage the cooking of puddings, I have done three further things in this book, which I hope will make the cook's life easier.

First, where I have found a good way of cutting corners, I have said so. It is surprising that so many pudding recipes still ignore microwaves and food processors; I use them often.

Secondly, I have tried to write the recipes to make them as easy as possible for the beginner. The instruction in a recipe to cream the butter and sugar is of limited use to a novice without some explanation of how to do so. Therefore, I have explained some basic techniques in Chapter 2, and included plenty of advice in the recipes, too, which I hope will be helpful.

Thirdly, I have generally set out a basic recipe for a type of pudding, and then a number of variations. Many pudding makers limit themselves to, say, a plain apple crumble, and then never go on to try an apple and raisin crumble or a rhubarb crumble. But they should.

Which pudding is best?

While discussing the joy of pudding one day with my Greek friend, Yiannis – who is both a foodie and a great fan of English puddings – he drew my attention to an essay by George Orwell, in which the writer complained that he was unable to obtain certain delicacies abroad. After listing kippers, Yorkshire puddings and so forth, Orwell continued with 'a list of puddings that would be interminable if I gave it in full: I will pick out for special mention Christmas pudding, treacle tart and apple dumplings'.

Everyone's shortlist of favourite puddings will, of course, differ greatly, and I would not follow George Orwell. But if you are puzzling over which recipe to try first, may I recommend a baker's dozen, in no particular order?

- Rice pudding with pudding wine
- Blackberry and apple crumble with custard
- Raspberry and blueberry crumble with custard
- Bread and butter pudding, straightforward and unvaried or with blackberries
- Sussex pond pudding with custard
- Steamed ginger and syrup sponge with custard
- Steamed chocolate pudding with chocolate sauce
- Steamed sticky toffee pudding

- Queen of puddings
- Apple tarte Tatin, perhaps with blackberries
- Treacle tart
- Blackberry and apple pie with custard
- Summer pudding

Finally, there is one further point I should make about the making of puddings. There are great delights in cooking for the busy person. It gives respite from the exercising of the brain. One is left alone by partners and children. It gives one time to listen to some music. It is satisfyingly creative in its own little way. And, most of all, the results give pleasure to the eaters of the pudding and, in particular, to yourself.

CHAPTER 2

Technical Matters

IN THIS CHAPTER I have attempted to be of some help to the less practised cook by offering a summary of useful equipment and important ingredients as well as essential techniques, which, once grasped, make one's time in the kitchen a great deal easier and more enjoyable.

Some useful hardware

Some sports, such as diving or flying, encourage the worst tendency in men to acquire gadgets, in particular those that are of limited use. Cooking puddings has rather fewer dangers in this regard; that is to say, there is plenty of useful kit, but it is not very expensive. Below I describe some basic pieces of equipment, most of them rather prosaic.

• *Blowtorch* ~ This is about the only really fun gadget you might want for cooking puddings. It is the key to a good crème brulée, which is almost the only thing you can make with it. You need a cook's blowtorch, not a big industrial one, otherwise you will burn away the whole pudding, if not the kitchen.

• *Cherry stoner* ~ This is very useful if you make puddings with fresh cherries, as it reduces the labour immensely. You might think it unnecessary, as it is in use for only a few weeks each year, but it can be used to stone damsons and olives, too.

• *Cups* ~ American and Antipodean recipes often use cups. A series of plastic cup measures, particularly a third and a half, can be useful for *outré* recipes from obscure colonial cookery books.

• *Microwave* ~ This is a useful implement for making proper custard. It is also good for heating up milk, cold coffee and old puddings and for melting butter. It has no other known uses.

• *Pie dishes* ~ These are usually Pyrex or ceramic, sometimes metal. Ones with very high sides are useful for baked puddings, crumbles, bread and butter pudding and milk puddings. I think pies, as with all pastry, are best made in metal dishes with relatively low sides. For pies, a lip is necessary, too, on which to fix the top and bottom together.

• *Pudding basins* ~ Traditionally, steamed puddings are made in ceramic basins.

They have a rim on the outside edge, which helps when attaching a cover. Finding very big ones can be a bit tricky, but they are useful if you want to make puddings in decent quantities, particularly because puddings can rise by up to a half, so you need to leave plenty of room. There are Pyrex and plastic alternatives, which are more than adequate.

• *Saucepans for steaming and boiling* ~ I have a lobster steamer. It is enormous and will take the largest pudding basin; it has a built-in floor with holes in it, under which one can have a pint or two of water boiling away without touching the bowl. An alternative pan that I have used is a *pastaiola*, a large Italian pot for cooking pasta. Otherwise, use a very large saucepan, with a lid of course. The saucepan obviously has to be rather larger than the pudding basin that will be put in it. You will need some form of rack or trivet to lift the bowl off the water; if you do not possess one, a saucer, or even a couple of forks, will do fine.

• *Scales* ~ You cannot easily survive without scales if you are making puddings. A rounded tablespoon of sugar is about 25g/1oz, and you can estimate how much butter you have by comparison with the packet (250g/9oz). But flour, for instance, does really need to be weighed. However, it should be said that one of the surprising things about recipes for most puddings is that you can find some that double or halve the quantities of quite important ingredients without any apparent harm to the finished product. Indeed, I am sometimes quite vague about quantities myself, suggesting 60–115g/2–4oz sugar, for example. In these cases, feel free to experiment, according to your taste. But while it is true that many puddings do not require precise measurement, beginners may not feel quite so confident, so scales are recommended.

• *Soufflé dishes* ~ These are for, well, soufflés obviously, but they are useful for other things – for instance, deep crumbles or bread and butter pudding.

• *Spoons* ~ The little ones are teaspoons, the middle size ones with which you eat pudding are dessertspoons, and the big ones are tablespoons. Teaspoons and tablespoons are often used for measuring. I tend to use proper calibrated ones, as ordinary spoons do vary in size quite a bit, but this is a bit unnecessary. A teaspoon is 5ml, a dessertspoon 10ml, and a tablespoon 15ml.

• *Tart tins* ~ These come in various sizes. Pastry cooks better in them than in china dishes. I think the best designs have loose bases, so you can just press up the base to remove the tart. This won't work so well for tarts that start very liquid, such as a chocolate tart, though if the pastry does not have holes in and you have a lipped metal plate in the oven under the tin you will not come to any real grief. Loose bases are hopeless for tarte Tatin, where the tart is cooked upside down on top of the filling, which would simply leak out. It is worth investing in a proper tarte Tatin dish, which is solid enough to withstand the initial caramelising of the sugar on the top of the stove. The last thing to say about tart tins is that if you are making pies, the tin needs to have a bit of a lip so that you can cement the top and bottom parts of the pie together.

• *Whisks* ~ A hand whisk is very handy for making custard. For most puddings it is useful to have a food processor for combining ingredients, and in particular for creaming butter and sugar together. You will need the whisk function or a separate hand-held electric whisk for a limited number of puddings where cream or egg whites need to be whisked, such as meringues and soufflés.

A note on some ingredients, what to buy and how to treat them

Puddings are made from simple ingredients: flour, butter, sugar, eggs, dried or fresh fruit and a few straightforward spices. I tend to go for the relatively expensive end of the range when it comes to chocolate and vanilla and the like. It's well worth it for the taste, and it's still pretty cheap compared with the price of beer.

• *Apples* ~ These are probably the most common fresh fruit used in puddings. You normally need cooking apples, such as Bramleys, although dessert apples can be used in tarts and pies. The difference between them is that cooking apples are larger and tarter and cook into mush; dessert apples hold their shape much better, and thus they are good (for instance) if you are making a tarte Tatin. These days, apples are available throughout the year. Apples are particularly good with cinnamon, raisins or blackberries.

• *Blackberries* ~ These are a perfect foil for apples, especially in crumble, but they are only available for picking for a short time around September each year. Bought commercial blackberries are expensive, and while they can be sweet and juicy, they don't have as much flavour or bite as wild ones. It is much better to pick them from the hedgerows, which, unlike golf, will not be a good walk spoiled. However, they do have prickles and a tendency to grow with stinging nettles (one must suffer for one's art). Blackberries do tend to go mouldy very quickly, so pick them for immediate use or for freezing, which they do very well. I normally put several old ice cream containers of blackberries in the freezer in September and use them throughout the year. If I can be bothered, I freeze them separately on a baking tray first, so that one does not have to unfreeze a block of blackberries when you want to use them. Try blackberries and apples together as a crumble, pie, Charlotte or tarte Tatin. If you get bored of blackberries and apples in September, try blackberries and pears instead, in any of the above or in a frangipane tart. Blackberries go very well in bread and butter pudding, and I have even used them to make a soufflé.

• *Breadcrumbs* ~ Many steamed and baked puddings are made with breadcrumbs. They are probably best made with day-old bread, but you can leave out some slices of fresh bread for half an hour to dry a bit instead. After the crusts are cut off and the bread roughly cubed, chop it up in the food processor until it resembles, well, breadcrumbs. I tend to make twice as much as I need and keep the rest in the freezer; they seem to keep very well. However, breadcrumbs should be allowed to thaw on their own. If you defrost them in the microwave, as I once did, you will end up with a nasty, coagulated mass.

• *Butter or margarine* ~ Margarine just does not taste the same, even in puddings. I don't think it much matters whether you use salted or unsalted butter: try it and see which you prefer. If you insist on using margarine, it needs to be the hard stuff sold for cooking, not soft.

• *Chocolate* ~ Plain dark chocolate has an obvious use in various chocolate puddings. Do look at the cocoa solids in the chocolate, which should be over 50 per cent, and preferably well over. What is described as cooking chocolate often has very little cocoa, and is much less good. Milk chocolate has a limited place in cooking, although using it in some recipes produces something that children are more likely to eat. A combination of, say, two-thirds dark chocolate and one-third milk chocolate is pleasantly acceptable to adults and children alike. Normally, one does not want solid bits of chocolate in the pudding, so it has to be broken up. You can grate it, or chop it up finely in the food processor. Alternatively, chocolate can be broken up into squares and then either melted over a gentle heat, or microwaved for 30 seconds at a time until done.

• *Cocoa powder* ~ This is used in quite a lot of chocolate recipes. It's worth buying good stuff. Drinking chocolate is not an adequate substitute. Ready-made chocolate sauce is often a rather good alternative, at least for children.

• *Cornflour* ~ This is useful for thickening, in particular for custards. It is NOT the same as ordinary flour, and can be found in small cardboard boxes in the baking section of the supermarket.

• *Cream* ~ I generally use double cream, and I specify it for most of the recipes in this book. Whipping cream is fine for most purposes. Single cream won't thicken when whipped, and is of more limited use. Avoid UHT like the plague, as it tastes funny. I am very partial to using crème fraîche instead of cream as an accompaniment to many puddings, at any rate if there is no custard.

• *Damsons* ~ These are effectively small and very intense plums. They are inedible raw, and delicious cooked. They need a bit more sugar than plums do. Stoning them is a bore without an olive/cherry stoner.

• *Dried fruits* ~ Apricots, currants, raisins, dates, figs, prunes and sultanas are often used in puddings. I tend to keep a large supply in my store cupboard.

• *Eggs* ~ Yes, you've guessed it, free range. They do taste better. And they do not trouble the conscience. I don't think the size of an egg matters much, as puddings are not haute cuisine requiring exact measurements, although the recipes in this book have a standard medium-sized egg in mind.

• *Flour* ~ When a raising agent is needed, for instance in steamed puddings, I generally use self-raising flour rather than adding baking powder to plain. (Little men who live in toadstools use elf-raising flour.) As I am lazy, I normally buy 00 or superfine flour to avoid having to sift it, which is otherwise essential. Plain flour is needed for crumbles, pies and tarts. Wholemeal plain flour is particularly good for crumbles, though I think one ideally wants a mixture of wholemeal and ordinary plain flour to prevent its being too heavy.

• *Fresh fruit* ~ This is the heart of crumbles, tarts and pies. If you are idle like me, one thing to bear in mind is how much preparation the fruit takes. Blackberries and raspberries require no more than a bit of picking over, as they tend to come dehulled, i.e. with the stalk already taken out. Strawberries can be easily dehulled just by slicing off the top, which is quick but slightly wasteful. Rhubarb only requires cutting up. Gooseberries need topping and tailing, which is a bore. Fruits that require stoning, such as plums, apricots and cherries, are a bit more of a pain. A cherry stoner is a good investment if you eat a lot of them. Some fruits, such as apples and bananas, turn brown if the flesh is exposed to the air for too long; this can be avoided by sprinkling them with a little lemon juice.

• *Garlic and vegetables* ~ I used to think that as garlic works in almost all savoury dishes, it would be worth seeing what it was like in rice pudding. I tried, and it was disgusting. (I tried a similar experiment with my eldest son, then aged three. He wanted tomato ketchup on his croissant, so I let him, thinking this would finally put him off ketchup with everything. Unfortunately the experiment failed, and he liked the combination, although he has not yet asked to put ketchup on any puddings.) Similarly, vegetables, generally, have a limited place in puddings. But there are honourable exceptions. Carrots (see p. 77) and sweet potatoes (see p. 159) can be used, and I have seen parsnips in some recipes. Rhubarb is officially a vegetable, which explains why it needs so much sugar, but I tend to refer to it as a fruit, as it is normally treated as one.

• *Jams* ~ Needless to say, go for some good ones. Homemade jams do tend to be best. A good indicator of a proper jam is that it has only two ingredients: fruit and sugar. I recommend the WI stall in any market if you want to get good jam.

• *Lemons* ~ Organic, unwaxed lemons are the best, as often the zest (the outer yellow skin) is needed as well as or instead of the juice. The white pith, which is between the zest and lemon itself, is rarely used. A lemon juicer is helpful.

• *Nutmeg* ~ This spice is very commonly used in puddings. You can buy it ground, but it does not keep well, and I think it is better to get whole nutmegs and grate them with a fine grater when needed.

• *Nuts* ~ Ground nuts, in particular almonds, are a common ingredient in puddings. Other nuts used include hazelnuts, pecans and walnuts. The very keen grind their own. Ground nuts do not last that long, though, so grind only as much as you need.

- *Plums* ~ They are particularly good for crumbles. You can leave the stones in, but this is far from ideal; then again, stoning can be a bit time-consuming. I think the easiest way, at least if the fruit is not so ripe that it falls off the stone, is to cut bits off the plum, say about an eighth at a time, leaving the stone with some small amount of fruit still attached.

- *Raspberries* ~ Perhaps my favourite fruit, they are particularly good in crumbles and summer puddings. They are very good in combination with blueberries.

- *Rhubarb* ~ This requires a special mention on its own, as it is pretty well my favourite fruit (even though it's a vegetable – see above) for many hot puddings, after blackberries. This is a taste I acquired in part thanks to Nigella Lawson's books, which have quite a few recipes involving rhubarb. It has recently been rediscovered by cooks and has become somewhat trendy. If you have a garden of a reasonable size, you can grow your own, and it requires very little attention or management. Only use the stalk; the leaves are poisonous. Spring rhubarb tends to be rather better than the stuff from later in the summer, and smaller stalks are preferable. Rhubarb is normally improved by adding a bit of ginger or orange, particularly orange zest. It contrasts nicely with oranges or lemons. It is surprisingly good with strawberries.

- *Spices* ~ These have a relatively short shelf life, certainly no more than a year. The standard ones for puddings are: cloves; cinnamon; ginger; mace; nutmeg (see above); and vanilla (see below).

- *Strawberries* ~ Surprisingly, they take on a much more intense flavour when cooked. They do tend to go a bit pappy in texture, so one does not want to cook them for too long. I often use strawberries (with other fruit) in crumbles or tarts. Many people have an aversion to cooked strawberries because of the texture; I think that this is much less of a problem if the strawberries are being eaten with some other fruit, such as rhubarb, which is a particularly good combination.

- *Suet* ~ I always use the stuff in packets from supermarkets. I do not know anyone who cleans and shreds their own. The alternative vegetarian stuff is actually perfectly all right if you are feeding vegetarians, though not perhaps quite so good as the real thing.

• *Sugar* ~ Granulated or caster sugar, whether white or unrefined, is used in most recipes. Brown sugars provide a different and distinctive flavour, useful for many recipes, whether demerara, light or dark soft brown, or light or dark muscovado. The latter in particular has a strong taste, which can overwhelm other flavours. Pudding obsessives like me have tins of different types of sugar, neatly labelled. Different people have varying views about how much sugar to use in a pudding, and you should experiment for yourself. Too little sugar, and a pudding is dull; too much and the other flavours are lost.

• *Treacle* ~ This is a trap for the unwary. Golden syrup, commonly used in puddings, is often known as treacle. For instance, treacle tart is made from golden syrup. It should not be confused with black treacle or molasses, which are much stronger and very useful in small quantities in a quite limited number of recipes. If I mean golden syrup, I will say so.

• *Vanilla* ~ Jolly important stuff, this, because it is necessary in custard. It comes in various forms. Chemical vanilla essence should be avoided, as it tastes odd. Vanilla extract is much better, and I use it all the time; it is moderately expensive, but it does last. Vanilla paste is also very good. It has the advantage over vanilla extract of having seeds, so your custard will have pretty little black bits in it (if you care about such things). Vanilla pods are very expensive, several quid each for little packets that often say 'may contain the produce of more than one country'. They dry up after a while. They need to be fat and sticky when you use them. You can make vanilla sugar by putting one in a jar of sugar for several days, and it is best just to leave the vanilla pod steeping in the sugar, as the sugar comes and goes, until it dries out after a couple of months and can then be replaced. You can scrape the little seeds inside into custard. In Sweden I have come across prepared vanilla sugar, which is very intense and made with icing sugar; in this country it tends to be quite expensive.

And finally...

• *Pudding wine* ~ This is the perfect accompaniment to a pudding. Cheap ones almost invariably are fine, and will do more than nicely if wine is needed in the pudding. Of course, nothing beats a good, old Sauternes (note use of comma). If one goes to the trouble of making a pudding, one might as well consume it properly: with pudding wine, and, of course, with custard.

A useful list of basic ingredients to keep in the cupboard

A serious pudding person may want to have the following available. The only thing on these lists that may be at all difficult to obtain is vanilla extract, but you can find that in large supermarkets.

Store cupboard – most useful
• Almonds
• Chocolate (dark)
• Cornflour
• Dried fruits: currants, raisins, sultanas
• Flour: self-raising and plain
• Golden syrup
• Spices: cinnamon (ground or whole), ginger (ground), nutmeg (ideally whole)
• Suet
• Sugar: caster, light brown, light muscovado
• Vanilla extract

Other useful possibilities for the store cupboard and freezer
• Almond extract (not almond flavouring)
• Baking powder
• Blackberries (frozen)
• Breadcrumbs (frozen)
• Dried fruits: apricots, dates, figs, prunes
• Flour: wholemeal
• Nuts, whole or in pieces: almonds, hazelnuts, pecans, walnuts
• Orange water and rose water
• Pudding rice
• Pudding wine
• Spices: ground or whole cloves, mace, vanilla pods
• Sugar: dark brown, dark muscovado
• Tinned fruits, e.g. cherries
• Treacle (black)

Fresh, normally for the fridge
Obviously, one buys fresh ingredients for each pudding, but the following are needed a great deal; so if they are always in your fridge, you will always be prepared to make a pudding:

- Apples
- Bread for breadcrumbs
- Butter
- Cream
- Eggs
- Lemons

Some basic and not-so-basic techniques
Making puddings is easy, but to help the nervous beginner, here are a few basic techniques that crop up regularly.

Boiling a pudding in a cloth
This is only needed for a few boiled suet puddings, and is described on p. 66.

Buttering a bowl
This is to stop the pudding sticking to the bowl too much. Use the paper from a block of butter and move the paper around the inside of the bowl, butter side down, until there is a very thin transparent layer of butter covering the bowl.

Creaming butter and sugar
This is useful in order to make steamed and baked sponge puddings, but it is not essential. Put the ingredients in a food processor, preferably chopping the butter into half a dozen or so pieces. It is best, I think, to start with hard butter from the fridge; the butter should not be too soft. Combine for quite a long time until the ingredients resemble solid cream. The texture will look a bit creamy and the colour should have gone a bit whiter than what you started with. If you go too far, the mixture starts to look a bit funny, with the butter beginning to melt. This is not a disaster, and you can still use the mixture. Creaming by hand is tedious work, and to be avoided. Creaming can be wholly avoided by melting the butter and mixing in the other ingredients; I add half a teaspoon of baking powder along with self-raising flour to ensure the sponge has sufficient lift. Some cooks may disapprove of such a short-cut, but it works very well for me.

Dissolving cornflour
Cornflour is useful as a thickening agent, for instance in custard. If it is added to a liquid, particularly a hot one, it can be difficult to dissolve and go lumpy. This can be avoided by adding to the cornflour a small quantity of cold liquid

(water or milk) at a time, stirring it in. The cornflour will turn first into a thick paste, and then into a liquid. It can then be added to the hot liquid or other ingredients. Some people think that cornflour ruins the flavour of custard. I do not think this is true provided not too much is used, and the main thickening agent is the egg yolks.

Folding

As the name suggests, you fold one ingredient into another to get them to combine without breaking them up mechanically. It is particularly important for introducing egg whites into a pudding mixture, but is also used for adding flour. Egg whites are whisked so that they are full of air bubbles, which expand a little when cooked and provide the raising agent for some puddings. When whisked egg whites are added to a pudding mixture, you do not want to lose all the air bubbles, so the whites are gently folded into the pudding, rather than whizzed in vigorously, which destroys them. It is probably best to fold with a metal spoon rather than a wooden one. Just pile the whites on top of the mixture, and mix in gently by using the spoon to scoop and turn the mixture. When flour is folded into a pudding mixture, it is far less important to ensure that the air is not beaten out of it; I tend just to whizz the flour in with a Magimix.

Preparing a basin for steaming a pudding

This is essential for steamed puddings. See p. 74.

Rubbing in

This technique is needed to make crumble and pastry if you don't have a food processor. Chop the cold butter into smallish pieces first and add it to the flour. Start by cutting the butter into the flour with two knives, drawn across each other like rudimentary scissors. When the lumps of butter are much smaller, rub in any remaining lumps quickly and gently with your fingertips.

Separating eggs

Separating an egg entails cracking it open and dividing the yellow yolk from the white. You will need two small bowls. Crack the egg gently against a hard edge, such as a bowl. Over a small bowl, prize the shell apart carefully at the crack, ensuring that the yolk remains in one half. Most of the white will then drip out into the bowl. Carefully pass the yolk back and forth between the two halves of the eggshell, until almost all the white has dripped into the bowl, and then put the yolk in a different bowl. If you are making a recipe that needs egg yolks and whole eggs, such as custard, it is a good idea to try to separate the eggs first, because if it all goes wrong and the egg yolk splits and drips into the white, you can use the resulting mess for the whole eggs, and then start again with the remaining eggs to get your yolks.

Sifting flour
If flour is to rise properly, it will need sifting to aerate it and to get any small lumps out. (It you buy 00 or superfine flour, it doesn't need sifting.) To sift, put one or two large tablespoons of flour at a time in a sieve over a large bowl. Either shake the sieve to and fro, banging it gently on the side of the bowl, or scrape the spoon gently round the sieve, until the flour has gone into the bowl. I tend to do this with the bowl on the scales, which have been zeroed with just the basin on them, so that I can measure the amount of flour needed.

Whisking (or beating), particularly egg whites
This is needed for a few, mostly light, puddings, but also for queen of puddings and lemon meringue pie. Whisking beats air into the egg whites, which provides the raising agent for some puddings, and it also turns them white (rather than transparent) and stiff. It takes a long time manually, but with an electric whisk it is pretty easy. Metal balloons are better for this than any plastic blades, which seem to take a great deal longer. Do not use a food processor with a normal cutting blade: this does not work and your egg whites will not stiffen up properly and the pudding will fall flat.

To whisk egg whites, separate the whites and yolks (see above), and put the whites in a large, clean, dry bowl. It is important that no yolk gets into the whites. Then whisk until the whites are stiff. You can tell whether the whites are sufficiently rigid because they will make little peaks. If necessary, stick a spoon in to see. The only difficult bit about whisking egg whites is to get the rigidity just right. You do not want the whites completely rigid, but only moderately stiff. Often, sugar will need to be added after the whites are whisked, and this is best done by adding 25g/1oz or so at a time, whisking after each addition of sugar to restore the whites to some rigidity. The first time you do this, it may not work properly, but you will soon get the hang of it. Whisking or whipping cream is much easier. There is no complication of trying to keep air bubbles, as the point is only to stiffen the cream. If it is to be added to some other ingredient, do not whip too stiffly, or it will be difficult to combine.

Zesting

The zest is the outer layer of peel on an orange, lemon or lime. The white pith is pretty inedible, and only the grated zest and the juice tend to be used in puddings. You can zest the fruit with a grater, ensuring that you remove most of the yellow (or orange or green) skin, but not taking off any of the white pith underneath. This is perfectly possible with an ordinary fairly fine grater, and I prefer it, but a proper zester is a fancy alternative. If the fruit is going to be juiced as well, do the zesting first, as it's difficult to grate an empty orange skin.

Quantities

Go for large quantities. Almost all puddings are good heated up again. If you go to the effort of making a pudding, normally to eat with other people at the weekend, you may as well have some left for private consumption later, particularly as you may not have time to make a proper pudding in the week.

Besides, the indications in many recipe books of the number of people that can be fed with each dish are often risible; the authors must have sparrow-boned mice in mind. I routinely double the quantities of many puddings that I make compared with the average recipe. I try to give in my recipes any adjustments that need to be made to the cooking time for larger or smaller quantities. It is important to ensure that you have bowls of sufficient size; you will need 1.7-litre/3-pint bowls or even larger for steamed puddings.

It is not always possible to make huge quantities of some puddings, such as crumbles, tarts and pies, where, for technical reasons, doubling the quantity does not work so well. In these cases, I tend to make two puddings at once and cook them in separate bowls or tins. You can always keep one in the fridge or freezer for hungry moments. With pies and tarts, you can use tins of 28–30cm/11–12in in diameter rather than the smaller 20cm/8in ones, but they can be a bit difficult to handle. I tend to use a couple of intermediate-sized ones of 23–25cm/9–10in.

I give an indication in each recipe of the number of portions one might expect to get from a pudding, if one is moderately realistic. But if the eaters are particularly hungry, this won't be accurate.

Weights and measures

I have given imperial and metric measurements for all ingredients. Again, you should not get too hung up about precise weights. The relative proportions of different ingredients vary markedly: you only have to compare the same pudding in a number of recipe books to see this. Thus, if you need about 2oz of sugar, which is 60g, 50g will normally do just fine. Greatly varying the proportions of ingredients does lead to a different outcome, but which you like best can be determined only by experimenting.

Temperature

Here is a temperature conversion chart. It is approximate and not exact. When a recipe says cook something for one hour at 160C, this is only a guide. It depends not only on the oven and where you put the pudding (top shelf, middle shelf, etc.), but also how big the pudding is, whether you make it thin (when it cooks more quickly) or fat (so the reverse is the case) and how cooked you like it. Puddings need to be tested to see if they are ready and will come to no harm if you do so (save for soufflés). About the only important point to note is the temperature for a fan oven: this should be about 20C less than the recipe states, and it may be a good idea to stop behaving like a man and read the instruction manual to see what reduction should be made for your oven. It can make quite a lot of difference for, say, a rice pudding.

Degrees Fahrenheit	Degrees Centigrade	Gas Mark
Very cool		
225	110	¼
Cool (milk puddings)		
250	125	½
275	140	1
Moderate (default setting)		
300	150	2
325	165	3
Moderately hot (crumbles, tarts, pies)		
350	180	4
375	190	5
Hot		
400	200	6
425	220	7
Blisteringly hot		
450	230	8
475	240	9

CHAPTER 3
Custard

THE ADDITION of custard makes a good pudding perfect. And it can be eaten on its own, of course. So it is surprising that very few people, even serious pudding fans, make their own. I think the reason is that the traditional way of cooking custard on the hob takes a long time, requires almost constant attention and is very easy to ruin if the custard is not caught in time. Fortunately, there is an easier way to do it. The trick to making custard easily is to use the microwave. I don't think I have ever seen this recommended in a cookery book, and I don't know why it is not used more widely. It might be thought that a microwave cooks unevenly, but if the custard is taken out of the machine every minute or so and stirred, it should almost always work.

Instant or bought custards are not a substitute for the real thing. They tend to be too sweet and to taste too much of cornflour. Crème Anglaise a l'Oiseau is a bit better, but not good enough. (Not everyone agrees with me. The Pudding Club, most of whose judgements I greatly respect, serves Bird's custard rather than proper egg custard.) An editorial in *The Times* in 2004 described custard as 'hot, sweet, comforting, sickly, addictive, vaguely toxic-looking stuff', and alleged that powdered custard 'is one of the few convenience foods that tastes as good as the real thing'. Wrong on both counts. Perhaps the editor had never tried proper custard.

My Basic Custard Recipe

This should be enough for at least dozen or so greedy people when eaten with pudding.

600ml/1 pint milk
600ml/1 pint double cream
1 vanilla pod (optional)
3 tsp cornflour, dissolved in 1 tbsp
  cold milk

1–3 tsp vanilla extract
4 eggs
4 egg yolks
115g/4oz white sugar

1. Put the milk and cream in a big enough serving bowl. Microwave on full power until nearly boiling (about seven minutes).
2. If using a vanilla pod, split it lengthways with a knife, scrape out the inside liquidy-grainy bits and add both the inside and outside to the mixture.
3. Meanwhile, combine all the other ingredients in a smaller bowl in no particular order.

4. Add this mixture to the hot cream and milk, stirring with a whisk.
5. Microwave the custard on full power for a minute at a time and stir with a whisk at the end of each minute, including after the last minute. It is likely to take between five and 10 minutes for the custard to cook.
6. Remove the vanilla pod before serving.

A note on quantities
The quantities above are for 1.2 litres/2 pints of custard. If you are making 600ml/1 pint, the only difference, save for halving the quantities, is that much less time will be needed in the microwave – about four rather than seven minutes initially, after which I do each minute of cooking with the microwave on half power.

Preventing the custard from separating
About the only difficult part of making custard this way is to tell when it is done. It should be getting quite a bit thicker, but not have gone grainy or granular. If it has started to do so, whisk vigorously – this will normally sort the problem out. Even if you have overcooked the custard and it has gone grainy, it will taste absolutely fine. You will soon get the hang of it.

A couple of other tips
First, if you are using a particularly powerful microwave, making smaller quantities or just feeling cautious, the last few minutes should be at half power. Secondly, if you make the custard in a thick container, it may continue cooking after it is removed from the microwave. This can be counteracted by putting the bowl in a basin of cold water and stirring the custard, or using a plastic bowl.

Hot or warm? Skin or no skin?
These are some of the pressing issues of our time. I don't think custard should be served hot. It should be less hot than the pudding, so that there is a contrast in temperature as well as taste and texture. The custard will therefore need to cool down for 10 or 15 minutes. Alternatively, make the custard an hour or two before eating it, and then warm it up in the microwave for a couple of minutes just before eating. If you choose this option, it is best to stir the custard every minute in the microwave to avoid overcooking the bits near the edge.

This leads to a difficult and much debated issue: skin or no skin? I like skin. Indeed, my Oedipal conflicts with my father were fought out over the custard and rice-pudding skins. But I recognise that most people don't share this view. Skin can be avoided in two ways. The best method is to put some clingfilm on the custard immediately after it has cooked. Alternatively, mix the skin into the custard a minute or two before eating. It should mostly dissolve into the custard, and if it leaves some lumps, that is what many custard-lovers like best of all.

Variations in method

• *Alternative microwave method* ~ You can simply add the ingredients to the cold cream and milk and heat them all up together.

• *Cooking on the stove* ~ I think that this is time-consuming and boring, as the mixture needs stirring most of the time with a wooden spoon. Also, it can be difficult to catch the custard in time before it curdles. This method is made much easier if you use a small electric whisk instead of a spoon. Start by heating the creamy milk in a saucepan until it starts to simmer. Pour over the other ingredients, and mix well. Return to the saucepan and simmer gently until the custard thickens, whisking (or stirring) all the time.

• *In the oven* ~ This makes a different type of set custard (see p. 28), which is not suitable for pouring on puddings.

Variations in basic ingredients

There are many. For instance:

• *Cornflour* ~ Purists do not use cornflour, as it taints the flavour of the custard. I don't think it does, provided you don't use too much. If omitting cornflour from my recipe, it would be a good idea to add another couple of egg yolks.

• *Cream or milk* ~ Some make custard with just milk or just double cream. If using only milk, it should be full fat, and it would be advisable to add a couple more egg yolks.

• *Eggs* ~ Try more or fewer eggs to see how it tastes. For crème brulée I tend to use eight egg yolks for 600ml/1 pint of custard and double cream rather than milk, though this is a bit extreme for pouring custard.

• *Vanilla extract* ~ If you are less fond of vanilla than I am, try one teaspoonful. Don't use vanilla essence, which tastes of chemicals.

• *Vanilla pods* ~ This is really just for looks; vanilla extract has much the same taste. The grainy inside bits will make pretty black dots in the custard (at least I think so; some think it looks like fag ash), but you can get the same effect with vanilla paste.

Interesting additions to custard

These are also legion. Several I have come across seem to be nasty in principle, such as carrot (a puréed carrot or two, use brown sugar and add cinnamon or ginger), mint (a handful of chopped mint) and coffee (a small cup of very strong coffee). I cannot bring myself to try these. But the following are definitely worth making, and I think are quite pleasant. They can be eaten on their own, or used for a suitable pudding (e.g. chocolate custard over chocolate pudding, lemon custard with steamed lemon curd sponge).

• *Bananas* ~ After making the custard, add about two and a half mashed or sliced bananas and mix in reasonably well. Leave for at least a few minutes to impregnate. Don't add very hot custard to the bananas or they will taste a bit cooked. I think this dish is much better eaten at room temperature rather than cold. Children normally love this, and so do grown-ups; it is serious comfort food.

• *Butterscotch custard* ~ Substitute the white sugar with light brown. Start by melting the sugar with about 60–85g/2–3oz butter (per 600ml/1 pint) for a few minutes in a saucepan over a low heat. Add to the hot cream/milk mixture along with the eggs and cornflour and continue as before. You may want to omit any vanilla.

• *Chocolate* ~ Add up to 2 tbsp of cocoa powder per 600ml/1 pint milk. I think it is better to add proper chocolate, about 115–170g/4–6oz per 600ml/1 pint. This can be milk (for children) or plain (for adults), though I think either a third to two-thirds or half and half are ideal combinations. Finely grate, chop or (best of all) melt the chocolate and mix in well to the cooked custard.

• *Coconut* ~ Replace up to half of the milk/cream with coconut milk.

- *Ginger* ~ Add about 1–2 tsp powdered ginger to the custard mixture per 600ml/1 pint. Alternatively, try some chopped fresh ginger, though it will have to be removed before eating (which is very difficult). You may wish to omit the vanilla.

- *Lemon* ~ Add to the milk/cream mixture the grated zest of one or two lemons per 600ml/1 pint milk, and the juice of up to 1 lemon. Omit any vanilla.

- *Orange* ~ Add the grated zest of 1–2 oranges per 600ml/1 pint milk, or the grated zest and juice of one orange. A tablespoon of brandy or orange liqueur is a good addition. Omit the vanilla. An alternative is orange flower water.

- *Spirits* ~ Mix into the cooked custard 1–2 tbsp per 600ml/1 pint spirits, particularly liqueurs. I suggest Marsala. Brandy and whisky are also popular.

Baked Custard

This should feed up to six people.

This is very different from ordinary custard because it is set rather than being runny enough to pour. It is eaten on its own, rather than as an accompaniment to other puddings. I sometimes have baked custard as a second pudding when people are coming to dinner, particularly rhubarb custard or Sauternes custard.

300ml/10fl oz milk	6–8 egg yolks
300ml/10fl oz double cream	1 tsp vanilla extract
60–85g/2–3oz caster sugar	Nutmeg to dust on top (optional)

1. Heat the oven to 325F/160C/gas mark 3.
2. Combine the milk and cream and heat in the microwave for about four minutes until hot but not boiling.
3. Meanwhile stir the sugar, egg yolks and vanilla together and whisk these ingredients in to the heated milk and cream mixture.
4. Put the custard mixture in a flattish dish. Place the dish in a roasting tin that has at least 2.5cm/1in of cold water in it. Cook in the oven for an hour or so

until set. The custard should be firm, but not immobile. You can tell when this is so if you insert a knife and it comes out clean.

5. Dust some grated nutmeg on top, if you want to.
6. Leave to cool before eating.

Some tips

Cooking the custard in a dish surrounded by water in a roasting tin prevents the custard from heating up too much. It is a good idea to try to have the top of the water near the same level as the top of the custard, otherwise the top and bottom of the pudding can cook at different rates. I tend to use boiling water, in which case the cooking time will need to be reduced to about 30 or 40 minutes. The easiest way to avoid the common problem of water spilling all over the kitchen floor is to put the roasting tin in the oven with a little water in it, add the custard in its dish, and then top up the water in the tin with a kettle.

I think this pudding is best eaten at room temperature or slightly above, when the custard is smooth and silky, rather than chilled, when it is a bit claggy. You can always make the custard a few hours in advance of eating it and then put it in a very gentle oven for 10 or 20 minutes to warm up again.

Variations

Generally I think you can use pretty well whatever ingredients you would for pouring custard, and you could, for instance, have milk and no cream, or replace some of the egg yolks with eggs. It is a good idea, though, to have more eggs or egg yolks than for pouring custard.

• *Orange or lemon* ~ You can mess about with baked custard just as you can with pouring custard. Most obviously, just add the grated zest of an orange or a lemon to the custard mixture (but omit the nutmeg and vanilla).

The next two I have adapted from Nigella Lawson's recipes and I greatly recommend them.

• *Rhubarb custard* ~ Chop 900g/2lb of rhubarb into pieces 2.5cm/1in long and gently cook with an extra tablespoon or so of sugar and a very small amount of water until it is a bit pulpy, about five or 10 minutes. Drain off the liquid then mix the rhubarb into the uncooked custard mixture and cook in the normal way, surrounded by water. The mild pink, early-season rhubarb is particularly good, both for the mild taste and the colour of the pudding. It is truly delicious. Tougher, later-season rhubarb is much less good for this pudding. I think a teaspoon of ginger mixed in before cooking is a good addition.

• *Sauternes custard* ~ This is seriously good. Replace the milk/cream mixture with 400ml/13fl oz cream and 200ml/7fl oz Sauternes, or preferably a cheaper dessert wine (I think using real Sauternes is a bit of a waste of a good wine).

• *Apple custard* ~ Mrs Beeton suggests a dozen large apples for 600ml/1 pint of custard, though I think about a third of this is better. Peel, core and cut the apples into quite small pieces and place them at the bottom of the dish, perhaps sprinkling them with some dark muscovado sugar. Cover with the custard mixture and then cook as above. The pieces of apple tend to float to the top a bit, and they stay whole rather than going mushy.

Crème Caramel

This should feed up to half a dozen people.

This is just baked custard with caramelised sugar underneath, and jolly delicious. Variations on this pudding are well known on the continent – for instance, Spanish flan.

85g/3oz granulated sugar	60–85g/2–3oz caster sugar
1–2 tbsp water	6–8 egg yolks
300ml/10fl oz double cream	1 tsp vanilla extract
300ml/10fl oz milk	

1. Heat the oven to 325F/160C/gas mark 3.
2. Mix the granulated sugar and water in the saucepan, bring to the boil and boil steadily until a golden colour.
3. Pour this caramel syrup into the base of a large baking dish.
4. Mix the cream and milk and heat in the microwave for about four minutes until hot but not boiling.
5. Meanwhile, stir the caster sugar, egg yolks and vanilla together. Whisk these ingredients into the heated milk and cream mixture.

6. Gently pour the custard mixture on top of the caramel syrup.
7. Place the dish in a roasting tin that has at least 2.5cm/1in of cold water in it.
8. Cook in the oven for an hour or so until set. The custard should be firm but not immobile. To check, insert a knife; if it comes out clean, it is cooked.
9. Leave to cool before eating.

Some alternatives

As with baked custard, the ingredients can be varied (for instance, use some whole eggs), and the same tips apply. You may wish to increase the amount of sugar if you want a lot of the brown gloop at the bottom of the custard after cooking. Instead of caramelising the sugar in a saucepan and pouring the molten mixture into a dish, you can use a tarte Tatin dish, if you have one. The sugar can be caramelised in it on the hob, and then the same dish can be used to cook the pudding in the oven.

Crème Brulée

This should be enough for up to six people.

Despite its French name, any Englishman will claim that this pudding was invented at Trinity College, Cambridge. It certainly appears in many old British cookery books from the 18th century, but this is some time before it was supposedly invented at Trinity in the 19th century. It is, perhaps, not big and substantial enough to count as a proper pudding, but it is basically custard, so I think it counts.

Crème brulée appears daunting because making egg custard is supposed to be difficult, and burning the sugar on the top can be tricky. However, it is easier than it might sound. The custard is not difficult to make with a microwave, and you can make baked custard in the oven instead. The top is easier to burn correctly if you use a cook's blowtorch, which makes good crème brulée and is great fun.

600ml/1 pint double or whipping cream
8 egg yolks (yes, I mean it)
60g/2oz sugar for the custard

2 tsp of vanilla extract
6 tbsp caster or demerara sugar for the top

1. Make the custard following the basic custard recipe on p. 24. The mixture should be quite thick; this is supposed to be set rather than pouring custard.
2. Put the custard in individual ramekins or one big flattish bowl and allow to cool. This will need half an hour in the kitchen to get the pudding cool enough to put in the fridge, and then about an hour in the fridge.
3. Sprinkle the sugar over the top of the stiff custard. The layer should not be too deep, but all the pudding must be covered.
4. Burn with the blowtorch. This takes quite a while, as you have to do one bit at a time. The sugar should turn into a brownish glaze. If it is too burnt, it will be very dark brown or black; personally I quite like it like that, but most people don't.
5. Put the pudding back in the fridge for at least half an hour and then eat. Do not leave for longer than a few hours or the brulée may go soft. With a big brulée rather than individual ones, you will need to tap the top in order to crack and break it up before serving.

Variations in method
· *Grill* ~ If you do not have a blowtorch, the sugar can be browned under a grill. This does tend to lead to some parts being burnt while others are still unmelted.

· *Hob* ~ Melt the sugar in some water and cook it gently on the hob until caramelised. The melted sugar can then be poured on to the cold custard.

Variations in ingredients
· *Whipping cream* ~ It is better to use whipping cream rather than double cream, as the latter makes the pudding quite heavy.

· *Lemon* ~ Add the grated zest of a lemon when heating the cream or cooking the custard, but it then should be strained later to remove the zest.

· *Vanilla* ~ The use of vanilla is not classical in crème brulée, but I think it is a good addition. The dots from a vanilla pod are quite pleasing.

Other additions
You can use any of the variations in ingredients that you could for normal pouring custard (see above), for instance adding some brandy, grated lemon zest

or cinnamon. If you use brown sugar instead of white sugar in the custard, you get a very good butterscotch crème brulée.

• *Alternative base* ~ Instead of custard, you can use a wholly different base, such as yogurt, whipped double cream or crème fraîche. This should be mixed with fruit (say bananas, blackberries, grapes or raspberries), with roughly twice as much base as fruit. You can, of course, mix fruit into an ordinary custard mixture instead. There is a serious danger that a cream mixture will melt when the sugar on top is brulée, so it is better to caramelise the sugar first and pour it on top.

• *Chocolate* ~ Try adding about 125g/4oz of dark chocolate. This needs to be grated finely and laid on the bottom of the dish before the custard mixture is added, which should then be baked. You could use a similar quantity of white chocolate instead, adding it to the custard mixture before cooking.

• *Rice pudding* ~ For a more extreme variation, use rice pudding instead of custard.

What to do with egg whites
One problem presented by excessive custard-making is the residue of unused egg whites. I put them in little bowls in the fridge, preferably labelled with the number of egg whites, and they stay there until they are either used or (more often) go off. There are several uses for spare egg whites. Some light puddings include them, such as Pavlova or raspberry soufflé (see Chapter 13). Or you can make little meringues. This is particularly popular with children, who can colour them green or purple with food dye. Macaroons are another use for egg whites. As meringues and macaroons are not proper puddings, I have not included a recipe here, but Nigella Lawson has good recipes for both in *How To Eat*.

CHAPTER 4

Milk Puddings

IN A POEM by AA Milne, no one could fathom what was wrong with Mary Jane, particularly as there was lovely rice pudding for dinner again. My daughter, when aged five, worked out what the problem was immediately, but then she never has liked rice pudding, not even mine. As the poem suggests, this pudding is very redolent of childhood, but not always in a good way, mostly because it is so often badly made. Personally, I liked my school's rice pudding, although it was probably not much different to that produced by most other institutions. Tinned rice puddings are just as bad: they are generally pappy and thin with a metallic taste, although I do not recall minding this when I was a teenager on cycling holidays and ate the rice pudding straight from the tin with a tyre lever. A good rice pudding, though, is an almost entirely different kettle of poissons, and it is very easy to make.

Rice puddings are common in other cultures. I have eaten rice pudding around the world, and the small and intense rice puddings of Turkey and Thailand particularly stick in the memory. Rice pudding was important in Buddha's life. After practising severe austerities, he ate some, and soon afterwards he attained enlightenment. In what other religion does pudding provide a fulcrum to the story? There was no pudding at the Last Supper, as far as we know, and certainly none is mentioned by any of the gospel writers.

The intense rice puddings of the Middle and Far East point us towards what one needs to make a good one. The requirements are, I think: (1) rich ingredients, in particular some cream instead of milk, or at least full-cream milk; (2) a very long cooking time, three hours at least for a 1.2-litre/2-pint pudding; (3) the use of spices. But people do have different views about how creamy a rice pudding should be, how firm or mushy they like the rice, and whether there should be skin (on which note, see below).

The real beauty of rice pudding is that it is ridiculously easy to make. Basically, you combine the ingredients of rice, milk and sugar, which takes a minute or two, and cook for a long time.

Basic Rice Pudding

This should feed up to about eight people.

85g/3oz pudding rice or risotto rice
85g/3oz caster or granulated sugar

1.2 litres/2 pints full-fat milk
Spices (see below)

1. Combine the ingredients in a (preferably buttered) pudding dish.
2. Place the dish in a preheated oven at 275F/140C/gas mark 1 for three hours.
3. Try to give it a stir every half hour or hour for the first couple of hours.
4. Eat on its own, or with cream, or even golden syrup. Easy, eh?

Minor variations in ingredients to make a very good pudding

• *Generally* ~ The proportions I have given above are pretty approximate. I have read recipes that suggest, for instance, 115g/4oz rice and 40g/1½oz sugar for a 1.2-litre/2-pint rice pudding.

• *Cream and butter* ~ I often replace up to half the milk with some double cream. I sometimes add 25g/1oz butter as well or, more usually, instead. If you are cooking the pudding for five hours, then cream and butter is certainly a little *de trop* and it can give you a slightly unappetising layer of fat on the top of the pudding, which can be stirred back into the mixture at the cost of losing the skin.

• *Semi-skimmed milk* ~ I often find I have semi-skimmed milk to use up, and one can make a perfectly decent rice pudding with it, but it is a good idea to add 25g/1oz or so of butter to increase the fat content, or replace 300ml/10fl oz of the milk with double cream.

• *Evaporated milk* ~ As an alternative to milk or cream, use evaporated milk, made up with water, but reduce the sugar by half.

• *Spices inside* ~ I like to put a vanilla pod in the pudding (or some vanilla extract, or use vanilla sugar), or a cinnamon stick (or 1 tsp ground cinnamon; though a piece of cinnamon bark is best of all). Any pod or stick should be removed before eating.

• *Spices on top* ~ I think grating nutmeg on top is vital, and it makes a good skin. You can use already grated stuff. To keep the nutmeggy skin intact, I normally add it only after the last stirring of the pudding (although if the skin is stirred in only a little bit, it does tend to rise to the top again later).

• *OTT spices* ~ The most elaborately spiced recipe I have come across has (for 600ml/1 pint of rice pudding) a vanilla pod, 4 tsp rose water and 1 tsp ground cardamom pods, as well as two handfuls of chopped pistachio nuts scattered on top before serving.

• *Rose water or orange flower water* ~ I have tried rose water in addition or as an alternative to other spices. It may not be to everyone's taste. Orange flower water is on the same lines. Both of them are quite faint tastes, so add more than just a mere dash, at least several teaspoons.

• *Bay leaf* ~ Another alternative is a bay leaf (which also needs to be removed after cooking).

Other mild variations in quantities and method
• *Quantities* ~ If a smaller pudding is required, you can halve the ingredients and reduce the cooking time a little bit. I sometimes make two separate rice puddings of 600ml/1 pint each, one for now and one for later, with slightly different spices.

• *Longer cooking time* ~ The longer the cooking time, the better. Five hours at 250F/120C/gas mark ½ improves the pudding. You may need to add about 300ml/10fl oz milk after about three hours, and in consequence the mixture should not be too rich to start with, so don't use too much cream, or just use milk. Reducing the cooking time by increasing the temperature is, in my view, a big mistake.

• *Quicker rice pudding* ~ If you are in a bit of hurry, you can boil (or at any rate heat) the mixture before transferring it to the oven, either on the hob or preferably in a microwave; this should reduce the cooking time by about half an hour or so.

• *Rice pudding on the hob* ~ If you cook the pudding from start to end on the hob, this will take about half an hour in total.

• *Skin* ~ This is controversial. I like skin, and thus always cook the pudding uncovered. If you do not want skin, cover the pudding; there will then be no need to add more milk.

• *Standing time* ~ Some (like my mother) suggest assembling the rice pudding and letting it sit for half an hour before putting it in the oven. With great respect to such an experienced pudding cook, I do not think it makes any difference.

Some more extreme variations

I am a little sceptical of most other variations to rice pudding. Many of them seem to be attempts to cover up its taste. I used to think that if you don't like rice pudding, then don't make it and don't eat it. However, I have become less extreme in middle age, and even I think that there are some variations that are acceptable and, in some cases, quite delicious. The quantities given below are for 1.2 litres/2 pints rice pudding.

• *Chocolate* ~ Add about 2 tbsp cocoa powder and perhaps a bit more sugar. I have tried twice as much cocoa powder, but that is a bit strong for the normal target audience, which is children. Ideally the cocoa powder should be blended with boiling water before it is added to the mixture. Alternatively, add grated or melted chocolate, which tastes rather nicer, I think.

• *Coconut, lime and cardamom* ~ Replace half the milk with coconut milk and the other half with double cream. Add half a dozen crushed cardamom pods and the juice of a lime or two.

• *Eggs* ~ Beat about three eggs into the mixture before cooking, or about 10 minutes before the end of the cooking time. Or use, say, two eggs and two yolks. (Mrs Beeton suggests four eggs a pint!)

• *Honey and almonds* ~ This is based on a medieval version of the pudding. Before cooking, stir in about 60g/2oz runny honey instead of the sugar and add 115g/4oz ground almonds to the mixture, as well as a couple of teaspoons of cinnamon. Serve with more runny honey, if wanted. It is best to think of honey in weight rather than volume, because one man's tablespoon is another's dessertspoon, given how much the honey sticks.

• *Jam* ~ This is for children, I think, and in my view it destroys the taste of the rice pudding. I am told that tart jams like apricot or blackcurrant are best, and that the jam should be stirred in only to streak the pudding.

• *Lemon* ~ Add the grated zest of two lemons and/or the juice of one. Add the zest before cooking, but mix the juice in after cooking, when the rice pudding has cooled down a little. Particularly if not overdone, this can be a refreshing change to ordinary rice pudding, and it does not destroy the original taste. Orange zest is a similar variation.

• *Muscovado sugar* ~ Replace the sugar with the same quantity of light or even dark muscovado sugar. This is a very distinctive taste, and spices are not really called for in addition, save perhaps for some nutmeg grated over the top.

• *Pudding wine* ~ This is wonderful. Melt about 60g/2oz butter over a low flame, add the rice and stir in, then add a third of a bottle of pudding wine, preferably Muscat, and let it reduce on a higher heat for a few minutes. Then combine the other ingredients (milk and sugar) and cook in the normal way, although for slightly less time, as the rice has already cooked a bit.

• *Sago and tapioca* ~ These can be cooked just like rice pudding, save that you will need to double the quantities of sago and tapioca. While I like them, be warned that sago and tapioca ('frogspawn') are less popular than rice pudding, so choose your recipients with care.

• *Sultanas, etc.* ~ Add about 115g/4oz currants, raisins or sultanas. You will need to reduce the sugar by about half. Mrs Beeton has a recipe for rice pudding that adds currants or sultanas, along with eggs, beef marrow (yes, really, but I have not tried it), brandy and lemon zest. Another alternative includes adding the same amount of dried apricots, chopped up a bit.

Semolina

This will feed about four people.

This takes much less time to cook than rice pudding, but it is a little more complicated to make. The slightly gritty texture is not to everyone's taste, but a substantial minority of people, including me, loves it. You can, of course, simply follow the instructions on the packet and cook the pudding entirely on the hob.

600ml/1 pint milk
60g/2oz semolina
60g/2oz sugar

1 tsp vanilla extract
Some grated nutmeg

1. Set the oven to 325F/160C/gas mark 3.
2. Bring the milk to the boil on the hob.
3. Add the semolina, stirring in well with a whisk, and cook for 10 minutes on a low flame until the mixture has thickened a little. Stir occasionally to prevent lumps from developing.
4. Take off the hob, add the sugar and vanilla and transfer into a ceramic bowl. Grate the nutmeg on top.
5. Cook in the oven for about 30–40 minutes.
6. Eat on its own, or with a dollop of jam, or some stewed fruit.

Variations

Semolina does need a bit of geeing up, more so than rice pudding. The possibilities are much like the variations for rice pudding, for instance:

• *Almond* ~ Try 1 tsp almond extract instead of the vanilla.

• *Butter* ~ Add 60g/2oz melted butter to the pudding, along with the sugar, after taking the semolina and milk off the hob.

• *Eggs* ~ Allow the semolina and milk to cool for five or 10 minutes after taking it off the hob. Add one to three beaten eggs to the mixture before putting the pudding in the oven. The effect of adding the eggs is to turn the texture rather more cakey. For a slightly souffléd effect, separate the eggs, mix the yolks together and then into the mixture, whisk the whites until they are reasonably stiff, and fold into the pudding. Reduce the cooking time to about 20 minutes.

• *Lemon* ~ Finely grate the zest of a lemon and add to the mixture with the sugar, omitting the vanilla and nutmeg.

• *Sugar* ~ Try replacing some of the sugar with light or dark muscovado sugar.

• *Sultanas* ~ A handful or two of sultanas considerably improves this pudding.

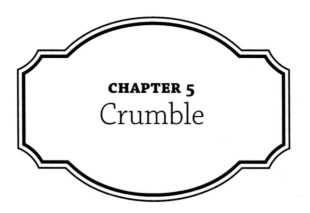

CHAPTER 5
Crumble

THIS IS THE BACH of puddings, suitable for all seasons and all men (and women), but also for the pudding connoisseur. Yiannis, my large Greek friend, when he was a serious rower at university, won a crumble-eating competition. I think he had 24 helpings, with custard. He also won the prize for the tidiest eater. He still likes crumble.

Crumble is an extremely simple pudding. The top is ridiculously easy to make and can be assembled well in advance and put in the fridge or freezer. I sometimes make double the quantity and put half in the freezer for the odd hungry moment weeks later. If the fruit needs preparation and any cooking on its own, this can also be done in advance and put in the fridge.

It is also quite quick. When assembled, the fruit and crumble cook in not much more than three-quarters of an hour. With staggered meals for children and grown-ups, I have made crumble in little ramekins for the children, which cook in 15–20 minutes, and used the rest in a bigger pudding for the grown-ups later. Crumble is particularly good for children: it gets the fruit bats to eat some stodge and the fruit-averse to eat some fruit.

As a result of all these things, I make crumble more often than any other sort of pudding, and I have given more variations for this recipe than for any other. I tend to think that apple, rhubarb and plum are the three basic crumbles, and I will set out recipes for them, with numerous variations, before listing assorted other types. But first, there are a few general issues to consider.

Some tips: quantities, thick or thin, squashed or not?

I like large quantities of crumble, as with any pudding. However, if you are making a lot, I suggest that you use at least two dishes to cook it in. If you make a very large pudding in one big bowl, the crumble is likely to be thick and it will be wudgy in the middle. I used to like thick, wudgy crumble, but I now prefer it to be very thin, which increases the relative proportion of the best bit, which is where the fruit and the crumble topping meet in a caramelly mush. I like the whole pudding, fruit and crumble combined, to be an inch deep, no more. This controversy about thick or thin crumble is much like that over thick or thin pizza; you will form your own view.

The measurements I give below are for a conventional 2lb fruit and ½lb flour (900g and 225g respectively), plus butter and sugar, of course, which makes a reasonable size of crumble for about six people. I often make rather more, in a number of dishes. Bear in mind that the stronger the taste of the fruit, the more crumble you may want. Thus very pronounced tastes such as blackcurrant need rather more crumble to fruit. Another solution, which I often use, is to add an equal quantity of apples, which make a relatively neutral base, to raspberries, apricots or whatever.

As the name suggests, the top of a crumble should be crumbly. This is obviously increased by making it thin. However, it is important to make it correctly. The butter and sugar should be mixed in with the flour to make a crumbly mixture, either with a machine or by hand, and it should then be sprinkled over the fruit. I think that it is a mistake to press the crumble down onto the fruit; it compacts it so much that it is no longer crumbly.

If using a food processor, don't overdo it, as it will make the mixture too fine. Mixing by hand, which is called 'rubbing in' (see p. 18), is very satisfying, particularly for small children, who will be able to do this from about four years of age. I think that it is wholly wrong to mush the mixture too much, melting the butter and making a solid dough.

Variations in the topping
The basic topping I use is 225g/8oz plain flour, 115–140g/4–5oz butter, and 115g/4oz sugar. It can be subject to infinite variations. Here are some.

• *Alternatives to flour* ~ Try replacing about a quarter of the flour (more if you like) with porridge oats (which are better chopped into very small pieces in a food processor), coconut (e.g. for mango crumble), ground almonds, walnuts or other ground nuts. Walnuts are particularly good with apple crumble, and ground almonds are particularly good with plum.

• *Flour* ~ I like replacing half the flour with wholemeal flour, preferably quite coarse wholemeal.

• *Quantity of butter* ~ You can reduce the butter to 85g/3oz or increase it to 170g/6oz. Don't use more butter, or the texture will go wudgy.

• *Sugar* ~ The white sugar in the fruit or the topping can be replaced by light soft brown, dark soft brown, demerara or light muscovado sugar. If this is used in the fruit instead of the topping, it makes the juice more caramelly. Light muscovado sugar can be a bit overpowering, but obviously less so with stronger fruit. Personally, I generally prefer light soft brown or light muscovado sugar in the topping, and light soft brown in the fruit.

• *Spices, etc.* ~ Add a teaspoon or two of spices to the fruit, for instance cinnamon or ginger, or a teaspoon or so of grated lemon or orange zest.

Apple Crumble

To feed up to six people.

You can get apples easily all the year round, so this is a pudding that is literally suitable for all seasons. There are very many delicious variations. I think apple crumble ideally needs something else with the apples, such as raisins, nuts, spices or some other fruit, otherwise it is a little dull, so I have made some suggestions in the notes that follow the recipe.

For the crumble:
225g/8oz plain flour, half wholemeal
140g/5oz butter
115g/4oz sugar

For the fruit:
900g/2lb cooking apples (dessert apples are not ideal)
60–115g/2–4oz sugar

1. Combine the ingredients for the crumble in a food processor or by hand (see 'Rubbing in', p. 18). The result looks (or should look) a bit like fine breadcrumbs.
2. Peel, core and cut up the apples into roughly equal-sized pieces. so that they cook evenly. For a big cooking apple, each quarter should be cut up into at least half a dozen pieces.
3. Put the apples and sugar in the bottom of a pudding dish.
4. Sprinkle the crumble mixture on top.
5. Cook for about 45 minutes or so at 375F/190C/gas mark 5 (somewhere between 350F/180C and 400F/200C will do just fine), although start to look at it after half an hour. The top should be brown but not burnt.
6. Eat with custard. Cream is an alternative, or try ice cream, mascarpone or crème fraîche.

Variations in method
• *Cooking the apples in advance* ~ Put the apples in a saucepan with a couple of tablespoons of water and cook gently, stirring occasionally, until they start to go soft but not mushy. This takes about 10 minutes. It prevents the apples

from being undercooked. However, it is not necessary if the apples are cut into quite small pieces and the apple and crumble layers in the dish are quite thin.

• *Cooking time* ~ You will need nearer half an hour if you use two pie dishes. If you are making a big thick pudding, it may need more like an hour. To avoid burning the top, put the wrapper from a block of butter on the pudding, butter side down.

Variations on a basic apple crumble

Here are just a few suggestions. The additional ingredients need to be stirred into the apples.

• *Alcohol* ~ Add a few tablespoons of rum, Marsala, wine, whisky or whatever to the fruit. If you are also using raisins, sultanas or the like, which I think is a good idea, you can soak them in the alcohol first, but add all the liquid to the apples afterwards. Marsala is particularly good for apple crumble.

• *Cider* ~ Adding cider greatly enhances the fruit; you will need to add about 300–425ml/10–15fl oz. Try soaking the fruit in the cider for an hour or two to infuse before cooking. To avoid having the fruit swimming in liquid, boil the cider down until it is, say, one-fifth of its original volume. If you start the boiling first thing, it should be ready when you come to assemble the crumble. I think sultanas are a nice addition to apple and cider crumble.

• *Jam* ~ Replace the sugar with about 115g/4oz of jam; gooseberry, for example.

• *Lemon/orange* ~ Add the grated zest of a lemon and some of the juice, or the same of orange.

• *Raisins* ~ Stir about 85g/3oz of raisins (or sultanas) into the apples, but reduce the sugar to about 25–60g/1–2oz. Do add some spices as well.

• *Spices* ~ A couple of teaspoons of cinnamon go well with apple, or try nutmeg or even fennel seeds. If you use less, you cannot taste it. If using cloves, though, don't use too much: half a teaspoon is enough. The spices will need to be stirred into the apples.

• *Sugar* ~ If you are using just apples, try some light muscovado sugar with them to make them a bit more interesting.

• *Walnuts* ~ Replace a quarter or a third of the flour with shelled walnuts, which will need to be processed or chopped very finely. Nigella Lawson suggests a very fine variation of apple and walnut crumble, which I greatly recommend, where raisins and a few tablespoons of Marsala are added to the apples.

Additional fruits

• *Apple and apricot* ~ Use 450g/1lb of each fruit and about 60g/2oz of sugar.

• *Apple and blackberry* ~ Blackberry and apple crumble is perhaps the finest of them all. Use about two or three times more apple than blackberry. For 900g/2lb of fruit, add up to about 115g/4oz sugar.

• *Apple and mincemeat* ~ Use 450g/1lb of apples and the same of mincemeat. Shop-bought mincemeat often needs some juice or the zest of an orange or lemon to gee it up a bit. This is really just a mincemeat crumble made less intense by the apples. You can reduce the mincemeat and increase the apples if you prefer. I don't think it needs sugar added to the mixture, but if you disagree, add 25–60g/1–2oz of sugar.

• *Apple and plum* ~ This is a particularly good mixture, I think. Try 450g/1lb of each fruit and up to about 115g/4oz of sugar, and perhaps a teaspoon or so of cinnamon or 25g/1oz or so of ground or flaked almonds. The plums do, of course, need stoning and then cutting up a bit.

• *Apple and rhubarb* ~ Try 450g/1lb of each fruit and 25g/1oz or so of sugar. A little cinnamon helps, or the zest and juice of an orange or two.

• *Apple and strawberry* ~ Use 450g/1lb of each fruit and about 85g/3oz sugar. This pudding seems to go down particularly well with small children. It certainly tastes more of strawberry than apple, but the strawberry flavour is not too overwhelming. It is, of course, ecologically unsound to buy strawberries out of season as they have been air-freighted from abroad, and in any event they lack taste. Cooking, though, brings out their flavour.

Rhubarb Crumble

For up to six people.

Rhubarb makes a seriously good crumble. I prefer it with ginger. Some sugar in the fruit is essential, as rhubarb tends to be too tart on its own. There are several additions and variations one can usefully make to a basic rhubarb crumble, which I will come to.

For the crumble:
225g/8oz plain flour, half wholemeal
140g/5oz butter
115g/4oz sugar
For the fruit:
900g/2lb rhubarb

60–115g/2–4 oz sugar
25g/1oz butter (optional)
1 tbsp dissolved cornflour (optional)
1–3 tsp of vanilla extract or 1–3 tsp ground ginger (optional)

1. Combine the ingredients for the crumble in a food processor or by hand (see 'Rubbing in', p. 18). The result should look a bit like fine breadcrumbs.
2. Cut the rhubarb into small pieces, say 1cm/½in long. Combine with the remaining ingredients in a saucepan.
3. Heat gently for five minutes or so, stirring occasionally, so that the rhubarb has softened a bit and the butter has melted and the ingredients have combined. If you are not using cornflour, there is likely to be too much liquid for a crumble, so drain some of it off and use it as a sauce later.
4. Cook for about 45 minutes at 375F/190C/gas mark 5 (somewhere between 350F/180C and 400F/200C will do just fine), although start to look at it after half an hour. The top should be brown but not burnt.
5. Eat with custard, cream, ice cream, mascarpone or crème fraîche.

Variation in method
You can avoid the hassle of cooking the rhubarb on the hob if the rhubarb is young and cut into small pieces and the layers of rhubarb and crumble are relatively thin (see above on whether crumbles should be thick or thin). The only real disadvantage is that rhubarb produces quite a lot of liquid, so the cooked pudding can sometimes be a bit soggy underneath, though this is greatly reduced if the rhubarb and crumble are in thin layers.

Variations in ingredients

Where does one start? One might want to add a couple of tablespoons of cherry brandy, perhaps using some chopped walnuts in the crumble mixture.

• *Ginger* ~ While the easiest thing is to add a few teaspoons of ground ginger, you could use chopped root ginger, or ginger in any other form.

• *Raspberry jam* ~ Stir up to four rounded tablespoons of raspberry jam into the rhubarb, reducing the sugar by the same amount, before covering with the crumble mixture. This might sound a yucky combination, but it is in fact quite delicious: after all, you are only adding raspberries and sugar.

• *Sultanas* ~ Add 25–60g/1–2oz sultanas and reduce the sugar a little, say by 25g/1oz. This is an excellent mixture. The finely grated zest of an orange or lemon is a nice addition, as are some walnuts in the crumble topping.

Other fruits:

• *Rhubarb and apple* ~ A classic pairing; use 450g/1lb of each fruit.

• *Rhubarb and blackcurrant* ~ Replace a quarter or half of the rhubarb with blackcurrants; a good combination.

• *Rhubarb and clementine* ~ Add two clementines to 900g/2lb rhubarb before cooking. The clementines should be cut into eight pieces, and the skins left on.

• *Rhubarb and fig* ~ Replace a quarter of the rhubarb with fresh or dried figs, and add some ginger.

• *Rhubarb and plum* ~ If you catch some very late rhubarb, you can make this combination with English plums. Try equal quantities of each fruit. Add a teaspoon of ground ginger.

• *Rhubarb and strawberry* ~ Rhubarb and strawberries are in season at the same time, though the rhubarb season is, of course, longer. This is perhaps a surprising mixture, but the strawberry sets off the rhubarb well and cooking enhances its flavour, so it complements the rhubarb rather than being overwhelmed by it. After stewing the rhubarb and sugar, if you are doing that, add the strawberries, dehulled and cut into quarters. There is a cheat's way of preparing the strawberries: slice off the top with the stalk, which will lose a very small amount of the fruit, then cut into quarters. This avoids having to dig away in the strawberry to get out the hull. Try adding a teaspoon of vanilla extract (though you may lose the taste of this anyway if you drown the pudding in vanilla custard, as I do).

Plum Crumble

For up to six people.

This is one of the great crumbles. It is best in summer, but it is also a good use for the less satisfactory plums that are available all the year round from far-flung corners of the world, if you can stomach the air miles (which you might when plums are being flogged cheaply).

For the crumble:
225g/8oz plain flour, half wholemeal
140g/5oz butter
115g/4oz sugar

For the fruit:
900g/2lb plums
60–115g/2–4oz sugar, or try honey
1–2 tsp cinnamon (optional)*
Zest and juice of an orange (optional)*

1. Combine the ingredients for the crumble in a food processor or by hand (see 'Rubbing in', p. 18). The result should look a bit like fine breadcrumbs.
2. Halve or quarter the plums, removing the stones, and place in a pie dish. Or you could just chop around the stone, taking bits off, which I think is easiest. Mix in the sugar and optional ingredients, if using.
3. Sprinkle the crumble mixture on top.
4. Cook for about 45 minutes at 375F/190C/gas mark 5 (somewhere between 350F/180C and 400F/200C will do just fine), although start to look at it after half an hour. The top should be brown but not burnt.
5. Eat with custard, cream, ice cream, mascarpone or crème fraîche.

*By optional, I do mean optional: I quite often leave out the last two ingredients, but do experiment for yourself.

Variation in method

If you prefer a thicker sauce, try cooking the plums for about five minutes on the hob, particularly if they are not ripe. Remove some of the juice, stir it into 2 tsp cornflour until dissolved, then stir back into the plums.

Variations in ingredients

I have given quite a lot of the variations already in the rhubarb crumble recipe, but here are some more. As with any crumble, you can mix and match your fruit. I have tried, for instance, plum and pear. Try the following.

• *Damson* ~ I think of these much like plums, which of course they are, and they can be treated in much the same way. The problem with damsons is that they are quite small in comparison with ordinary plums and need stoning. A cherry or olive stoner is very useful, otherwise this process is a bit of a bore. Try adding a dash of gin to the damsons, about 1 tbsp per 450g/1lb fruit; too much and the damsons will be overpowered.

• *Greengages* ~ These are really just green plums and work well in a crumble.

• *Nutty toppings* ~ Nutty crumbles go very well with plums. Replace a quarter or half of the flour with finely chopped walnuts, pecans, macadamias or hazelnuts. I think almonds are good, too.

• *Plum and apple* ~ See apple and plum, above.

• *Plum and banana* ~ See bananas and other fruit, below.

• *Plum and raspberry* ~ This is a particularly fine pudding; try equal quantities of both fruits.

• *Plum and strawberry* ~ A good mixture; use equal quantities of each fruit.

• *Plum and rhubarb* ~ See rhubarb and plum, above.

Some other crumbles

This is by no means an exhaustive list. Many other fruits can be used, such as blueberries. I have made a very elegant cloudberry and white raspberry crumble, which is a bit difficult to do in this country as there are no cloudberries available; you would need to go to Finland in August near the Arctic Circle where the midges are the size of turkeys. Use 900g/2lb fruit, unless otherwise stated, with the crumble mixture given above.

• *Apricots* ~ For 2lb ripe apricots, use 25–60g/1–2oz sugar, and the normal crumble topping (as above). Cut the apricots in half or into quarters, and remove the stones. I think it is too fiddly to remove the skins. Drained, tinned apricots can be used instead, though they will need no or little sugar added. The crumble can be made more interesting by replacing a quarter or half of the flour with ground or chopped almonds: apricot and almond is a particularly good combination. Alternatively, replace some of the flour with crushed amaretti biscuits, or add 85g/3oz of crushed ratafia biscuits to the fruit.

• *Bananas and other fruit* ~ On their own, bananas are not a good choice for a crumble, as they are a little bland and pappy. However, they are excellent when combined with intense fruits. Try bananas with kiwis, strawberries, raspberries, plums or cherries, or a combination of all or any of these, and 60g/2oz sugar. The proportions can be about half to two-thirds bananas and half to one-third of the other fruit. Strawberries take on a much more intense flavour when cooked. Be warned that some people do not like cooked bananas.

• *Blackcurrants* ~ As they are very intense, reduce the fruit to 450g/1lb blackcurrants with about 60g/2oz sugar, to go with the normal topping quantities. Blackcurrants need to be stripped from their stalks before cooking.

• *Cherries* ~ This is a particularly good and intense crumble. Remove the stones before cooking. If you do not have a cherry stoner, the labour is intensive. About 675g/1½lb cherries is sufficient for the normal amount of crumble topping. Try about 85g/3oz sugar with 675g/1½lb cherries.

• *Compotes* ~ There exist good-quality commercial fruit compotes made only of fruit and some sugar. Using them is a good and easy way of making crumble, and they are of course available out of season. Thus, for instance, you can try apricot compote, using equal quantities of apples. Check the quantity of sugar in the compote; it will normally be sufficient, so no more sugar needs to be added to the fruit.

- *Dried fruits* ~ Apricots, prunes, figs or whatever can be used. Use 450g/1lb dried fruits in place of the usual 900g/2lb fresh fruit, but soak in 600ml/ 1 pint or so of water for some hours and preferably overnight, discarding the soaking water before adding.

- *Gooseberries* ~ You will need about 115g/4oz sugar for the fruit. They are likely to need topping and tailing. A plain gooseberry crumble is delicious, but try adding a few tablespoons of elderflower cordial and even a few tablespoons of double cream. Gooseberries goes well with strawberries – perhaps half and half of each fruit.

- *Mangoes* ~ Try about three mangoes, peeled and cut up, with about 60g/2oz light brown sugar and a teaspoon or so of cinnamon (or ginger, or ½ tsp nutmeg).You may want to add 115g/4oz blackberries, blueberries or some other small, intense fruit.

- *Peaches* ~ Fresh or tinned peaches make excellent crumble. If using tinned, drain and rinse and do not add sugar. Peaches go well with almonds, either in the fruit or as part of the crumble top. A dash of vanilla extract, well mixed in with the peaches, is a very good addition. However, plain peach crumble is just fine. I cut up the peaches somewhat roughly, keeping on the skin.

- *Pears* ~ This excellent crumble can be made all the year round, as pears are always available. They will need to be peeled, cored and cut into pieces. You can stew them first in a little water, though I don't bother. Add 60g/2oz sugar to 900g/2lb pears. Cinnamon is good with pears, as is ginger. Crushed walnuts are particularly good as part of the crumble topping. Pear and blackberry is a nice alternative to blackberry and apple crumble, if you have a glut of blackberries in September and want a change, though I just freeze as many blackberries as possible for use throughout the year.

- *Raspberries* ~ Reduce the fruit to 450–675g/1–1½lb fruit, rather than the usual 900g/2lb, for the normal quantity of topping. You can add a couple of thinly sliced ripe bananas. Redcurrants also go well with raspberries, and plum and raspberry is very good. However, the best combination I have found is raspberry and blueberry, which makes a particularly fine crumble.

Cobblers

Serves up to six.

And the same to you. Fruit cobbler is halfway between a crumble and sponge, and is the closest relation the Americans have to proper crumble. Before cooking, the topping looks more like pastry than crumble, though it has none of the difficulties of making proper pastry.

For the topping:
225g/8oz self-raising flour
115–140g/4–5oz butter
115g/4oz sugar
1 egg

2–4 tbsp milk or double cream
For the fruit:
900g/2lb of fruit, as for the crumbles
  above

1. Rub in the butter, flour and sugar as for a crumble. Beat the egg with the milk or cream, add to the dry ingredients and mix to form a soft dough.
2. Pat or roll out the dough so that it is about 1cm/½in thick.
3. Prepare the fruit as for a crumble.
4. Place the pastry on the fruit.
5. Cook as for a crumble – about 45 minutes at 375F/190C/gas mark 5.

Variations
• *Instead of rolling* ~ Just take globs of topping, squeeze them into flat pancakes and put them on the fruit in overlapping discs. This is particularly rewarding for small children.

• *A simpler cobbler* ~ If you omit the egg and milk, then you have a dry topping that can be used as for a crumble, the only difference being that the flour is self-raising rather than plain. Try a teaspoon of baking powder with plain flour to give a lighter texture.

Which fruit?
You can use any fruit, such as plums, peaches or whatever. I have made cobblers from, for instance, apples and pears.

CHAPTER 6

Bread and Butter Pudding

BREAD AND BUTTER PUDDING is really just a variation of baked custard (see p. 28) with some bread added. It is straightforward to make, does not need cooking for a particularly long time, and it tends to go down well even with those who are not proper pudding eaters. Nowadays, it is even quite fashionable. It also uses up large quantities of stale bread, if any is left over from feeding the ducks.

Bread and butter pudding suffers from much the same adverse publicity as rice pudding, no doubt from the same cause of bad experiences at school. An inadequate bread and butter pudding will have lots of bread, too little butter, cream, spices or fruit, and will no doubt be burned on top to boot. Properly made, it has none of these defects. Having said that, there are two schools of thought about how much bread there should be in comparison with all the other ingredients. I used to go for solid quantities of bread, with crusts on. A minority school of thought, which I now take more seriously than I used to, regards the pudding as an egg custard, with a few pieces of crustless bread floating in it. The latter is definitely worth trying. To do so, you probably will not have to reduce the normal quantities of the bread in the recipe below, as taking the crusts off will do that for you.

Bread and Butter Pudding

Makes enough for six reasonably solid people.

This recipe makes a moderately large pudding. I have sometimes doubled the quantity, and you can then cook it in two dishes if desired. Don't follow any of those recipes that suggest that a bread and butter pudding made of two slices of bread will feed a family of four; that's tosh.

115–170g/4–6oz butter, plus extra
  for buttering the dish
10–12 slices of white bread
115–170g/4–6oz sultanas
Grated zest of 1 lemon

6 eggs
900ml/1½ pints mixed double cream
  and milk, preferably half and half
115g/4oz caster sugar
Nutmeg

1. Butter a large (1.7-litre/3-pint or more) baking dish. This is easiest using the buttery side of the butter paper.

2. Butter each slice of bread quite thickly. It helps if the butter is quite soft.
3. Put a layer of the bread at the bottom of the dish, butter side up. Sprinkle generously with the sultanas and add some grated lemon zest. Repeat with layers of bread, sultanas and lemon zest. The final layer should be bread and should be well below the top of the dish, as the pudding rises when the custard mixture is added.
4. Make the custard mixture by beating the eggs lightly, and then whisking in the milk, cream and sugar.
5. Pour the custard mixture gently over the pudding. It takes a little time to soak in. There should be enough custard to just cover the pudding, but this can sometimes be a bit tricky to get just right.
6. Leave to stand for a few minutes, preferably for half an hour or even an hour, to allow the custard to soak in. Meanwhile put the oven on to 350F/180C/gas mark 4.
7. Grate (or sprinkle) some nutmeg over the pudding.
8. Put the pudding in the oven and cook for about 45–60 minutes. Test it by pushing a knife into the middle: the custard should be just cooked, and the top should be golden brown.
9. Leave to stand a little before eating, at least 10 minutes, so that it is warm rather than very hot.
10. Most people serve bread and butter pudding with cream. It might seem a little over the top to have custard, as there is lots already cooked into the pudding, but I think it is delicious.

Tips and variations in method
• *How to layer the bread* ~ To achieve an even layer of bread in the dish, it helps to start with pieces of bread that are cut into two triangles. You will normally have to cut off bits here and there to make the slices fit, and stuff odd holes with little bits of bread.

• *Heating the milk* ~ If you heat the milk before making the custard mixture, the pudding's standing time can be reduced. The milk should be warm and not boiling.

• *Lemon zest* ~ This can be added to the custard mixture, rather than sprinkled on each layer of bread.

• *Microwave* ~ Bread and butter pudding can be microwaved. A large one will need about 15 minutes. I don't really think it is quite as good, though.

• *Quantities* ~ I sometimes make somewhat larger puddings, normally in two dishes. If you are making a particularly big pudding, take care that it is properly cooked through in the middle. To avoid the crust burning, put some butter paper over the top.

Alternative method

Here is a very slappy-dippy way of making bread and butter pudding, which is great fun, and much liked by children in particular. Cut or break up the bread into rough cubes or squares of about 1cm/½in dimensions. Melt the butter (which is most easily done in the microwave, say 20 seconds at a time) and pour it over the bread. Add all the remaining ingredients and mix together with your hands (fun) or with a large spoon (boring). I think it is best if the liquid is added after it has been warmed up a bit. Sprinkle nutmeg on top. This method has the great advantage that it is easy to ensure you have the right amount of liquid for the pudding, and the right amount of sugar, as you can adjust the ingredients as you go along.

Variations in the pudding

These variations are not generally mutually exclusive. You can add almost anything to bread and butter pudding. Well, not quite anything: rhubarb, for instance, turns grey and flabby.

• *Alcohol* ~ Half a dozen tablespoons are quite enough, I think, and you may want less. Soak the dried fruit in brandy, Grand Marnier, rum, whisky or whatever for a few hours beforehand. Mix any excess alcohol into the custard mixture before cooking.

• *Apricot jam* ~ Spread 225g/8oz apricot jam thickly over the bread and butter before assembling the pudding. You can leave in the sultanas, but omit the lemon zest.

• *Apricots* ~ Chop up 225g/8oz dried apricots, adding 60g/2oz sultanas, and 300ml/10fl oz of pudding wine. Omit the lemon. Bring the mixture to the boil, and leave to soak for at least a couple of hours, if not overnight, so that the fruit is nice and soft. This can be stirred into the custard mixture. You can, of course, just use apricots, which you may wish to soak in water before cutting them up.

• *Bananas* ~ Add up to about four bananas. This is quite nice with, say, 115g/4oz dried apricots and the raisins, but without the lemon. Soak and chop the apricots and slice the bananas. Mix the sliced bananas, apricots and raisins, and sprinkle over each layer of bread. Be warned that some people do not like cooked bananas very much.

• *Blackberries* ~ Add about 225g/8oz blackberries and 60g/2oz more sugar, but omit the lemon, sultanas and nutmeg. I think this is best with crustless bread, and with the pudding made quite thin. It is a truly good variant, much to be recommended.

• *Bread* ~ You can replace the white bread with, for instance: banana bread; brioche (reduce the butter you use as a result); croissants (same point; jolly good); brown bread; French bread; pain au chocolat; panettone; or soda bread. If you have stale bread of any type, with the possible exception of olive bread, make a bread and butter pudding. If the bread has dried fruit in it, reduce or eliminate the dried fruit that is already in the ingredients.

• *Candied peel* ~ Add 25g/1oz or so of candied peel, sprinkling some on each layer of bread with the fruit. Like lemon, this gives the pudding some necessary zest, but it is not to everyone's liking.

• *Chocolate* ~ Use about 225g/8oz of chocolate, preferably good dark chocolate with at least 50 per cent cocoa solids. To make it more child-friendly, a mixture of two-thirds dark chocolate and one-third milk chocolate works quite well, and is still palatable to adults. I have tried using milk chocolate on its own, which is just about all right, and much liked by children.
There are essentially two ways of introducing the chocolate. The first is to distribute it equally throughout the pudding: either melt the chocolate and add it to the hot milk mixture, or grate it into the hot milk, then pour this over the bread. It is especially necessary to allow the pudding to stand for a good long time, or you will end up with white bits, unless you use the slappy-dippy method (above), which makes the integration of the chocolate much easier.

The second method is simply to sprinkle the grated chocolate over each layer of bread.

If you are adding chocolate, I think it is best to omit the lemon and dried fruit from the basic recipe, but you could use the grated zest of a lemon. Try adding some rum and cinnamon to the custard mixture, or some orange flower water. A very simple (if rather expensive) way of making chocolate bread and butter pudding is to use pain au chocolat.

- *Cinnamon* ~ Mix 1 tsp ground cinnamon into the custard mixture before pouring over the bread.

- *Coconut milk* ~ Substitute all or most of the milk with coconut milk. If you replace just some of the milk, the coconut flavour can get a bit lost. Add a few tablespoons of rum and omit the lemon. This might all sound a bit unappetising, but I think it is delicious and well worth trying.

- *Cranberries* ~ Invented by my son Nicholas when aged six, who turned up one Sunday morning with the recipe all written out (admittedly without cream and eggs). Just use dried cranberries instead of the sultanas, and don't add any lemon.

- *Crusts* ~ A smoother, more custardy pudding can be made by removing the crusts from the bread. It is easiest to butter the bread before cutting off the crusts.

- *Dried fruit* ~ You can use currants or raisins instead of sultanas, or even chopped dried apricots.

- *Ginger* ~ Mix in a teaspoon or two of ginger to the custard mixture before pouring over the bread. Or finely chop or grate 60–85g/2–3oz stem or preserved ginger and sprinkle over each layer. I know this sounds quite a lot, but the pudding will take a great deal of ginger. Indeed, I have tried using both ground ginger in the custard and grated ginger in each layer, with good results. It is best to omit the lemon and the spices from the normal recipe, though you may wish to leave in the sultanas. Ginger bread and butter pudding is sometimes known as Cluny pudding.

- *Lemon* ~ Some do not add any lemon zest to the pudding. I think this makes the pudding too bland, unless using some substitute such as marmalade or orange (below) or candied peel (above). I sometimes add the juice of a lemon as well as the zest.

- *Marmalade* ~ There are, to put it mildly, quite a lot of recipes for this. Basically, you just spread the bread and butter with marmalade before assembling the pudding, then complete it in the normal way. For the larger size of pudding I have suggested, I tend to add about a jar of marmalade, about 225g/8oz, which is quite strong; some recipes recommend half this amount. You can omit the fruit and lemon zest. I tend to replace the lemon zest with orange zest, but I do not think it has much of an impact because the flavour of the marmalade overpowers it. Candied peel can enhance the marmalade. If you keep the sultanas, soak them in some rum or brandy first, and add any excess alcohol to the custard mixture before pouring over the bread. Replacing some of the sugar with dark muscovado is good. I have made this pudding with dark muscovado sugar, evaporated milk and brown bread, which is delicious.

- *Mincemeat* ~ Add about 115g/4oz of mincemeat to the fruit, and spread over each layer of bread and butter.

- *Orange* ~ Replace the lemon zest with orange zest. Personally, I think that this is rather better than lemon.

- *Richness* ~ I like a rich pudding. You can make it less so by reducing the cream and increasing the milk, reducing the number of eggs, or buttering the bread less thickly. Or you can make the pudding even richer, for instance by using more eggs, mostly in the form of egg yolks, or more cream and less milk.

- *Sugar* ~ Replace the white sugar with, for instance, soft brown sugar.

- *Topping* ~ Try sprinkling a little demerara sugar over the top of the pudding with the nutmeg. Or replace with a little brushed apricot jam.

- *Vanilla* ~ I tend to add a teaspoon of vanilla extract to the custard mixture.

Bread Pudding

This should feed about 10 people.

There are dozens of versions of bread pudding. It is very popular in America, although many recipes for it closely resemble bread and butter pudding. Here is a basic English bread pudding. It is more like cake than bread and butter pudding. I tend just to throw in stuff in a very approximate way: this is not a pudding that needs anything in the way of precision.

675g/1½lb stale bread
600ml–1.2 litres/1–2 pints milk
 or water
350g/12oz mixed fruit
170g/6oz soft dark brown sugar

3 tsp spices (mixed, or whatever)
170g/6oz melted butter or suet
 (optional, but a good idea)
2 eggs (optional, but a good idea)
2 tbsp caster sugar (optional)

1. Break the bread up and soak it in the milk or water for about an hour or more. If you want it to soften more quickly, use breadcrumbs and hot water or milk. If you are using a lot of liquid, you may need to squeeze out the excess when well soaked.
2. Heat the oven to 350F/180C/gas mark 4.
3. Beat the bread well with a fork to get a creamy mixture, then add all the other ingredients save for the caster sugar.
4. Grease a large ovenproof dish with butter and add the bread mixture. Spoon the caster sugar on top.
5. Bake for one hour.
6. Serve with custard or cream.

Variations
There are a great many. For a start, the most authentic bread pudding probably does not have any butter or suet. You could add 115g/4oz marmalade, a chopped cooking apple, the zest of a couple of lemons, any combination of these, or some fruit.

CHAPTER 7

Boiled Suet
Puddings

SUET PUDDINGS are what kept the Royal Navy afloat in the Napoleonic era, which considering the solidity of the puddings is no mean feat. Boiled puddings have gone out of fashion, which I suspect is for logistical reasons. When cooking facilities were more basic, boiling was easy to undertake. Indeed, puddings could be boiled in a large pot along with the main course. But now, steaming or baking is just as straightforward, and many think it produces a better result. However, the boiled pudding has an essential clagginess and solidity that really should be tried. While most suet puddings can be either steamed or boiled (or, indeed, baked, which takes an hour or less), there are three that I think are much better when boiled: jam roly-poly pudding, spotted dick and cloutie dumpling.

How to boil a pudding

You need a cloth about 40cm/15in square, depending on the size of the pudding. Sheets and pillowcases (clean, obviously) are suitable, but I use tea towels as they are always around in the kitchen. The cloth is supposed to be scalded with boiling water first; I don't think this is necessary if it is clean. Having said that, traditionally the inside of the cloth is dredged in a little plain flour, so that the flour makes a skin on the pudding, which does require scalding the cloth first to make the flour stick. If the outside of the pudding looks wet and claggy after cooking, it can be dried off in the oven (10 minutes at the lowest possible temperature), perhaps after sprinkling with sugar.

Place the pudding in the middle of the cloth and tie it up, but not too tightly, as there needs to be a little room for expansion. I tend to make puddings in a cylinder rather than a ball. To secure the cloth, bring together the two long edges and loosely roll them over on themselves. Then secure them along the length of the pudding with safety pins. This needs to be done quite thoroughly, otherwise bits of pudding tend to escape. Ordinary pins are less satisfactory. The remaining loose ends of cloth can be tied with a piece of string, so that the pudding now looks a bit like a Christmas cracker. The length of string between the two ends can be used to lift the pudding in and out of the water. Or, if there is sufficient cloth left at the ends of the pudding, they can be tied together.

If you want to make round puddings, put the cloth in a bowl, add the pudding mixture, tie the cloth loosely at the top, and then attach some string to lift the pudding in and out of the boiling water.

The pudding should be completely immersed in the boiling water, which will need to be topped up from time to time. Place a plate upside down on the bottom of the pan, so that the pudding does not touch the bottom.

An alternative way to boil a pudding

Mrs Beeton's book includes recipes for quite a few types of boiled puddings. For most of them, she suggests putting the pudding in a basin, covering the top and then boiling the pudding in the bowl. To boil a pudding in this way, prepare the pudding and basin in just the same way as for a steamed pudding (see p. 74). However, it is a good idea to tie down the silver foil top with some string to avoid water leaking in. The pudding should be immersed in boiling water to within 1cm/½in of the top of the basin, and, of course, topped up with boiling water from time to time. This is an effective alternative to the traditional method of boiling a pudding in a cloth.

Boiled or steamed?

I once conducted a controlled experiment, in which I cooked two lots of Snowdon pudding (see p. 86), one by boiling (using Mrs Beeton's method) and one by steaming. They were noticeably different. The boiled pudding was whiter and more claggy, and the guinea pigs who ate the results preferred the steamed pudding, although, it must be said, only mildly. The great advantage to boiling such a pudding rather than steaming it is that boiling took rather less time, a couple of hours rather than three.

Cloutie Dumpling

This serves about 10 ordinary-sized people.

Effectively, this is the Scottish equivalent of Christmas pudding. I have never eaten it anywhere but at home, though I expect it can be found in Scotland. It is a seriously substantial pudding and is unbelievably easy to make. 'Cloutie' refers to the cloth in which the pudding is boiled.

350g/12oz plain flour
1–2 tsp baking powder
1–2 tsp ground cinnamon
1–2 tsp mixed spice
115g/4oz suet

170g/6oz sugar, white or brown
350g/12oz raisins, currants and
 sultanas
½ tsp salt
225ml/8 fl oz milk

1. Fill a large saucepan with water and start bringing it to the boil.
2. Mix all the dry ingredients together, and then add enough milk to bind the pudding into a soft (but not too soft) consistency.
3. Tie the mixture up in a pudding cloth (see above) and place in the saucepan of boiling water.
4. Boil for at least three hours, preferably four, then take out of the water. Check the saucepan at intervals to make sure it isn't boiling dry, and top up with boiling water from the kettle if needed.
5. After removing the cloth, dry off the skin of the pudding in the oven for quarter of an hour at a cool temperature. You can sprinkle sugar on the surface before drying it off.
6. Eat with custard, cream or ice cream.

A few variations
There is no standard recipe. Here are just a few variations.

• *Breadcrumbs* ~ Replace up to half of the flour with fresh breadcrumbs.

• *Butter* ~ Use butter instead of suet for a slightly lighter pudding.

• *Fruit* ~ Use raisins, currants or sultanas, or preferably a mixture of them. Try adding some dates.

• *Fruit and vegetables* ~ Add a carrot and an apple, peeled and grated.

• *Oatmeal* ~ Replace up to half of the flour with oatmeal.

• *Rum* ~ Add a couple of tablespoons of rum.

• *Treacle* ~ Add a tablespoon of black treacle or golden syrup.

• *Steam instead of boil* ~ This is not so authentic, but the pudding does tend to come out a bit lighter and takes much less time to cook. See 'Boiled or steamed?' above.

Jam Roly-poly Pudding

This will serve about eight people.

This pudding has a jam streak running through it, hence its tasteless nicknames of housemaid's leg and dead baby. It is not as heavy as cloutie pudding, but the frequent descriptions of it in old cookbooks as 'light' are somewhat misleading.

225g/8oz self-raising flour
115g/4oz suet
60g/2oz white or brown sugar
¼ tsp salt

150ml/5fl oz water or milk, as needed
225g/8oz jam, normally raspberry or
   strawberry

1. Fill a large saucepan with water and start bringing it to the boil.
2. Mix the flour, suet, sugar and salt together in a bowl, then add enough of the water or milk to bind the pudding into a dough.
3. Roll the dough out on a floured surface into a square or oblong. I tend to do this with my hands if the mixture is too sticky.
4. Spread the dough with a thick layer of jam, leaving a margin all the way around of 1cm/½in or so.
5. Roll up the dough like a Swiss roll. Dampen the edges of the dough with a little milk or water to seal them.
6. Tie up in a cloth (see above) and place in the pan of boiling water.
7. Boil for about two hours, then remove to a wire rack to drain briefly.
8. Unwrap the pudding, cut into slices and serve with custard and perhaps some jam sauce (jam gently heated on the hob, with a little water added to thin it).

Variations
• *Apple* ~ Instead of jam, try an apple filling, using two peeled, cored and chopped cooking apples, 60g/2oz each of currants and sugar, and a couple of tablespoons of golden syrup.

• *Jam* ~ I use 225g/8oz, but some double or halve the quantity according to taste.

• *Lemon* ~ Add the grated zest of a lemon to the jam.

- *Other alternatives to jam* ~ The jam can be replaced by the same quantities of marmalade, syrup or mincemeat.

- *Quantities* ~ I often increase the quantities by 50 per cent or more, which will require another half an hour's boiling.

- *Baked* ~ This pudding can also be baked. Wrap the pudding up in silver foil (rather than a cloth) and cook it on a baking sheet, or preferably in a roasting tin. It needs about an hour at 400F/200C/gas mark 6.

Spotted Dick

This will serve about eight people.

This pudding is also known as plum bolster (as it looks like a long pillow), raisin roly-poly, fly cemetery or spotted dog. Under the latter name it was beloved by Patrick O'Brian's Jack Aubrey. It is similar to jam roly-poly, but even easier to make.

115g/4oz self-raising flour	225g/8oz raisins, sultanas, currants
115g/4oz breadcrumbs	or a mixture of them
115g/4oz suet	¼ tsp salt
60g/2oz white or brown sugar	150ml/5fl oz water or milk, as needed

1. Fill a large saucepan with water and start bringing it to the boil.
2. Mix all the dry ingredients together in a bowl, and then add enough water or milk to bind the pudding into a dough.
3. Turn out on to a floured surface and roll into a log shape.
4. Tie the pudding up in a cloth (see above) and place in the pan of boiling water.
5. Boil for about two hours then remove to a wire rack to drain briefly.
6. Unwrap the pudding, cut into slices and serve with custard.

Variations
- *Quantities* ~ I normally increase the quantities greatly, often doubling them, which will mean that the pudding needs boiling for another half hour or so.

• *Brandy* ~ Soak the fruit in some brandy.

• *Breadcrumbs* ~ You can replace the breadcrumbs with self-raising flour.

• *Fruit* ~ Some recipes halve or double the quantities of fruit.

• *Lemon* ~ The grated zest of a lemon or orange is a good addition to the pudding.

• *Spices* ~ Add a teaspoon of ginger or cinnamon, or somewhat less of nutmeg.

CHAPTER 8

Steamed
Puddings

THIS CHAPTER IS the emotional core of this book; puddings to warm the soul. These are the Brahms of puddings: unshowy but well constructed; deeply satisfying; autumnal and slightly melancholy; suitable for middle age, like Trollope. Just as Brahms can be played adequately by an amateur orchestra, unlike, say, Mozart or Strauss, these puddings can be made by anyone. In particular, they are not very sensitive to being cooked too long, nor indeed to variations in the ingredients and quantities. You can, for instance, double the amount of suet in the recipes below without coming to any real harm.

Almost the only way I have ever managed to damage a steamed pudding at all was to allow all the water to boil away, which I have done a few times. It is obvious when this has happened because the kitchen starts smelling pretty nasty. Even then, leaving the burnt stuff untouched on the bottom of the bowl, I scraped off the top two-thirds of the pudding, which turned out to be quite unharmed and was thoroughly edible. (I did, however, once do this with a plastic basin at my mother's, and the pudding was unsalvageable, along with the basin and the saucepan. She was not pleased.) I recently managed to assemble a ginger and syrup steamed pudding and put it on to steam, when I realised that I had used plain flour instead of self-raising. I tried to mix in some baking powder, but after cooking it still looked like brown sludge. Nevertheless, it remains true that it is Really Quite Difficult to ruin a steamed pudding.

I have divided this rather long chapter into three parts. First, the heavy steamed puddings based on suet, to which flour or breadcrumbs are added, and where the ingredients only have to be mixed together. Secondly, steamed sponge puddings, where butter and flour are usually creamed together, and then flour folded in. Finally, a few breadcrumb puddings, which do not involve suet.

How to prepare a pudding bowl for steaming

This is, in fact, very straightforward. Do not be put off by the detailed instructions given below, which are intended to avoid any possible mishap. It takes only a couple of minutes to prepare the basin, and not much longer to assemble the pudding itself.

Prepare the covers of the pudding bowl first, before assembling the ingredients. Cut a circle of greaseproof paper or baking parchment to the size of the pudding bowl; it is best to upend the bowl on the paper, draw around the bowl and then cut. You can get ready-prepared circles of greaseproof paper, which makes this rather easier; if they don't exactly fit your bowl, it doesn't matter too much.

Then, to make the second covering, take a long length of silver foil, about three or four times as long as the diameter of the bowl. Fold it in half lengthways. Make a pleat in it by folding (still lengthways) near the centre, then fold back again 2.5cm/1in or so away from the first fold. This pleat allows some space for expansion.

Take another long length of foil of even greater length, and fold it lengthways twice, to make a strip about 5cm/2in wide; this is for lifting the bowl in and out of the boiling water.

Penultimately, butter the bowl with the paper from a block of butter.

Lastly, take your largest saucepan and put a trivet on the bottom (two or preferably three crossed forks will do fine). Put 600ml/1 pint or so of water on to boil. When you place the pudding above the trivet in the bottom of the pan, it should not quite get its feet wet, but it should be jolly close to the water.

Cooking the pudding

When the pudding mixture is made, transfer it to the bowl. It should not fill more than two-thirds of the bowl. Cover with the greaseproof paper. Place the silver foil lid on top of the pudding bowl and crinkle the edges tightly around the sides of the bowl. Place the bowl on the long silver foil handle and carefully lift it into the saucepan of boiling water, holding one end of the foil handle in each hand. Cover the saucepan with a lid.

The boiling water will need to be on a medium heat for half an hour or so while the pudding warms up, and after that it should be turned down a bit or the water will boil too vigorously and may boil entirely away. Check every now and then, but not in the first hour, to make sure there is sufficient boiling water. Top up if necessary with boiling water from the kettle.

About half an hour before the pudding is supposed to be cooked, take it out of the saucepan with the silver foil handle to see if it is nearly ready. Gingerly take off the silver foil wrap and the greaseproof paper. Poke a small sharp knife into the middle of the pudding to see if it is cooked: it should be relatively firm and not liquidy. If it is not cooked, cover the pudding again and put back in the saucepan. Repeat every 15 minutes or so.

Steamed puddings should be allowed to sit for a few minutes after cooking. I often find it best to have the pudding cooked before the meal; I then heat it up again in the saucepan of water for another 10 minutes or so before serving.

Sophisticated cooks will turn the pudding out before serving. While this is not strictly necessary, it makes it easier to cut up the pudding and extract slices to eat. Run a long palette knife between the bowl and pudding, place a large plate on the top, and upend the bowl on to the plate using a pair of oven gloves, firmly holding both bowl and plate. The pudding should then fall on to the plate. It is not uncommon to have some of the pudding stick to the basin, but the bits can usually be removed from the bowl and replaced on the pudding.

Some useful tips
• To help prevent the pudding from sticking, cut a small circle of greaseproof paper and place it on the bottom of the pudding bowl. This is particularly useful if you are making a pudding with jam or golden syrup on the bottom, but even then I don't tend to bother.

• If the silver foil is not on tight enough, you may find that steam leaks into the pudding. To be sure of avoiding this, tie some string around the lip of the bowl. You can then construct a loop over the top to make a handle. The only reason I don't like doing this myself is that it is very fiddly to check whether the pudding is cooked.

• If you use a plastic bowl with its own lid, grease the bowl and place some greaseproof paper under the lid, but you don't need silver foil as well.

• An alternative to steaming a pudding is to use a slow cooker, which can produce much the same result, because the temperature at which it cooks should be similar.

Steamed Suet Puddings
These puddings are undoubtedly solid, and perhaps as a result less popular than steamed sponge ones. But for a cold winter's day after a bracing walk, murdering pheasants or golf balls, nothing is quite as good. Custard is particularly important for such a pudding in order to balance its solidity. I have found that in principle many people think a steamed suet pudding is rather uncongenial, but when presented with some will eat it with gusto and ask for seconds. You are missing an essential pudding experience if you do not try steamed suet puddings. They are also extremely easy to make: you just mix up the ingredients any old how and cook. If you want to make the pudding a little lighter, add a teaspoon of baking powder.

A word on quantities

The basic pattern in these recipes is 225g/8oz suet and 225g/8oz of flour or breadcrumbs. This will make a reasonably substantial pudding, enough for, say, eight people. For a larger pudding, increase the quantities by half or double them, and cook for an extra half hour or so.

Carrot Pudding

This will feed about eight.

I have come across a number of recipes for carrot pudding, some of which use potatoes instead of breadcrumbs. This particularly appetising one is adapted from Mary and Debbie Smith's *Great British Puddings*.

225g/8oz breadcrumbs
115g/4oz suet
350g/12oz peeled and finely grated
  carrots
225g/8oz currants and raisins
85g/3oz light muscovado sugar

1 tsp ground cinnamon
4 eggs, lightly beaten
3 tbsp orange juice
3 tbsp sherry
2 tbsp milk

1. Prepare the pudding bowl and put a saucepan of water on to boil (see p. 74).
2. Mix the first six ingredients together. Add the eggs, juice, sherry and milk and stir well to mix.
3. Transfer the mixture to the pudding basin, and cover as described on p. 75.
4. Place a lid on the saucepan and steam for two and a half hours.
5. Eat with custard, of course.

Variations

This is even more adaptable than most puddings. For instance, you can use milk in place of the juice and sherry, try some other alcohol, replace the light muscovado sugar with white, substitute half of the breadcrumbs with self-raising flour, or half the carrots with potatoes, or the dried fruit with sultanas, or add 115g/4oz chopped nuts. This pudding can also be baked instead of steamed; bake for an hour or so at about 375F/190C/gas mark 5.

Christmas Pudding

This is enough for about three large puddings. My mother doubles these quantities!

This is my great-grandmother's recipe. I have been eating it all my life, and not just at Christmas. It is perfect. The pudding is, of course, very easy to make and cook. The only daunting thing is to assemble the very large number of ingredients (traditionally 13 of them to represent Christ and the Apostles). It needs to be cooked some time in advance of Christmas (see 'When to make' below).

575g/1lb 4oz raisins
350g/12oz currants
225g/8oz sultanas
225g/8oz mixed peel
225g/8oz apples, peeled and grated
350g/12oz plain flour
1 tsp salt
2 tsp mixed spice
350g/12oz fresh breadcrumbs
350g/12oz suet

225g/8oz caster sugar
225g/8oz soft brown sugar
170g/6oz blanched almonds, chopped
Grated zest and juice of a large lemon
Grated zest and juice of a large orange
At least 4 tbsp brandy, plus half a
 ladleful for igniting
At least 3 large eggs
Approx 150ml/5fl oz milk

1. Mix all the dry ingredients and the apples in your very biggest mixing bowl. (My mother uses a washing-up bowl for the huge quantities she makes.)
2. Add the lemon and orange juice, brandy, eggs and milk and mix in.
3. Cover with clingfilm and leave overnight.
4. Prepare the pudding basins. They need to hold about 2.25 litres/4 pints.
5. Stir the mixture again. This can be a family enterprise, with each person stirring and making a wish, starting with the youngest. If you have some very old coins, preferably clean ones, stir them in.
6. Fill the basins, and cover as described on p. 75. Steam for nine hours (five hours for a pudding half the size).
7. On the day, the pudding will need to be steamed for another five hours (a couple of hours for one half the size). You could use a slow cooker instead to free up the hob, which tends to be a bit crowded on Christmas Day.
8. Remove the pudding from the steamer and leave to rest for a little.
9. Take half a ladle of brandy and heat in a small pan on the hob. Scoop it up

into the ladle, light it with a match, then pour it over the pudding; it should stay alight. The flaming pudding should be brought into a darkened room for maximum effect.

10. Serve with brandy butter (see recipe below).
11. If there is any pudding left over for another day, it is particularly delicious if each slice is briefly fried in butter to heat it up.

Variations
I don't think that any variation is necessary, but other recipes vary the relative quantities enormously. For instance, the cooking time is often given as about half what I suggest (a terrible idea), and the eggs and brandy are often at least doubled. With the flambéed brandy, and bearing in mind the tastebuds of children, I do not think that much more than 3 tbsp brandy is necessary, nor do you need to 'top up' the pudding with brandy between making it initially and eating it some months later.

When to make
Traditionally, Christmas pudding is made on Stir-up Sunday, about five weeks before Christmas. The collect for the day starts with the words 'stir up' and thus reminds everyone to get cracking with the pudding. There is no harm in making it many months earlier. Christmas pudding keeps almost for ever, and my mother always makes one for the following Easter, as well as Christmas.

Brandy butter
This should be made on Christmas Day, or shortly before, but will keep for at least a week in the fridge. It is very straightforward and quick to make. Put equal quantities of sugar and cold butter into a food processor, say 115g/4oz of each. If you make double the quantity, there will be some left over for mince pies and seconds of Christmas pudding on Boxing Day. Use icing sugar, perhaps with some granulated sugar for the texture. Cream the butter and sugar. Then add brandy to taste, a tablespoon at a time and cream in thoroughly. You will probably need about three tablespoons in all. Put the brandy butter in a bowl and keep it in the fridge, as it needs to be cold when it is put on the Christmas pudding. There are countless variations of this recipe: some use other sugars, such as light brown, and add cinnamon or vanilla or even the grated zest of an orange, or replace the brandy with rum.

College Pudding

Sufficient for about eight people.

This is a good, solid and tasty suet pudding made with breadcrumbs and dried fruit. It supposedly derives from Oxford and Cambridge colleges, though I doubt it is cooked there any more.

225g/8oz white breadcrumbs
1 tsp baking powder
225g/8oz suet
225g/8oz currants, sultanas or raisins
115g/4oz soft brown sugar

25g/1oz candied peel
¼ tsp grated nutmeg
150ml/5fl oz milk and brandy, mixed
2 eggs, lightly beaten

1. Prepare the pudding bowl and put a saucepan of water on to boil (see p. 74).
2. Mix all the ingredients together, adding the eggs last.
3. Transfer the mixture to the pudding bowl, and cover as described on p. 75.
4. Place a lid on the saucepan and steam for about three hours.
5. Remove from the saucepan and, if desired, turn out after a few minutes' sitting. This pudding turns out more easily than many.
6. Eat with custard.

Variations

• *Method* ~ There are quicker ways of cooking the pudding: for example, bake at 350F/180C/gas mark 4 in moulds for 45 minutes or so; or drop small balls of the mixture into hot oil, butter or lard, and fry for about three minutes. The latter is recommended by Mrs Beeton, as is the brandy.

• *Brandy* ~ Use some other alcohol such as Marsala instead of the brandy.

• *Butter* ~ Use butter instead of the suet for a lighter pudding.

• *Dried fruit* ~ Use any mixture of raisins, currants and sultanas that you prefer.

• *Lemon* ~ Replace the candied peel with the finely grated zest of a lemon (I think that one or the other is needed to give the pudding a little tang).

• *Spices* ~ Instead of nutmeg, try 1 tsp cinnamon or ¼ tsp cloves.

• *Sugar* ~ Use caster or light muscovado sugar instead of soft brown.

Cumberland Pudding

Will serve eight or so people.

This is a suet pudding made with apples and dried fruit. It is apparently named after the Duke of Cumberland. Presumably he ate it after a hard day's work slaughtering Scotsmen. It is effectively a version of bachelor's pudding made with suet.

115g/4oz self-raising flour
115g/4oz fresh white breadcrumbs
115g/4oz suet
115g/4oz currants or raisins
85g/3oz soft brown sugar
Grated zest of a lemon

225g/8oz cooking apples, peeled, cored and cut into quite small pieces, or coarsely grated. This is about one large cooking apple.
Half a grated nutmeg
3 eggs, lightly beaten

1. Prepare the pudding basin and put a saucepan of water on to boil (see p. 74).
2. Mix all the ingredients together, adding the eggs last.
3. Put the mixture in the pudding basin, and cover as described on p. 75.
4. Place a lid on the saucepan and steam for about two and a half hours. Remove from the saucepan.
5. Eat with custard.

Variations
• *Flour* ~ The breadcrumbs may be replaced with self-raising flour.

• *Mixed peel* ~ The lemon zest can be replaced with 1 tbsp mixed peel, or more if you want.

• *No fruit* ~ Some recipes for this pudding omit the currants or raisins entirely. Increase the sugar by 60g/2oz to compensate, or add 2 tbsp golden syrup.

Fig or Herodotus Pudding

I have gone slightly over the top on this one, which should feed up to 16 ordinary people; you may want to halve the quantities.

This is sometimes called Herodotus pudding because the Father of History includes a recipe for it in his Histories (with raisins as well as figs, lemon, honey for sugar, and some wine in the pudding). It has a traditional association with Easter and Christmas, although the term 'fig' is often used to include raisins, currants and sultanas.

450g/1lb dried figs (yes, this is a lot)
225g/8oz fresh white breadcrumbs
225g/8oz self-raising flour
225g/8oz suet

170g/6oz light or dark brown sugar
4 eggs, lightly beaten
1 tsp each of nutmeg and cinnamon
3 tbsp brandy

1. Prepare the pudding basin and put a saucepan of water on to boil (see p. 74).
2. Chop or mince the figs; I do not think it matters much which. If you chop the figs in a food processor, they may well end up minced anyway.
3. Mix all the ingredients together. This needs a bit more mixing than most puddings because of the figs. The most efficient way to do it is with one's hands.
4. Transfer the mixture to the pudding basin, and cover as described on p. 75.
5. Place a lid on the saucepan and steam for about three and a half hours.
6. Eat with custard, or brandy sauce (see below).

Variations

• *Brandy sauce* ~ An alternative to custard is a brandy sauce, a mixture of 350g/12oz sugar, 115g/4oz butter, 2 tbsp brandy, 1 tsp vanilla extract, all gently heated or whizzed together and cooled in the fridge.

• *Breadcrumbs and flour* ~ Instead of a mixture of breadcrumbs and flour (which Mrs Beeton has for her fig pudding), try just breadcrumbs (as Mrs Beeton does for Herodotus pudding), or indeed just self-raising flour.

• *Figs* ~ Replace half the figs with dates and prunes, or raisins or sultanas.

- *Lemon* ~ I think the grated rind and juice of a couple of lemons, or indeed oranges, is a very good addition.

- *Milk* ~ The brandy can be replaced by milk or rum.

- *Spices* ~ Replace the cinnamon or nutmeg with cloves or mace.

- *Suet* ~ Some recipes for this pudding double the quantity of suet, or for a lighter pudding replace it with butter.

- *A richer pudding* ~ To make a richer, more Christmassy pudding, add (for instance) a peeled, cored and chopped apple or two, a cup or two of chopped nuts, some chopped prunes, or whatever.

- *Cooking method* ~ Instead of boiling, the pudding can be baked for an hour or so at 375F/190C/gas mark 5.

- *Quantities* ~ Halving the quantities makes a more normal-sized pudding for about eight people; reduce the cooking time to three hours.

Hampshire Six-cup Pudding

This will feed about eight.

The name comes from the fact that each of the six ingredients has the same volume. A cup was used to measure ingredients before many people had scales, a habit continued by our transatlantic cousins. It is much like Cumberland pudding (see above), but without the apples. I would, of course, recommend doubling the quantities given below: after all, the recipe does not say how large the cup has to be.

115g/4oz self-raising flour
115g/4oz fresh white breadcrumbs
115g/4oz suet
115g/4oz soft brown sugar

115g/4oz currants, raisins or sultanas,
 or better a mixture of them
150ml/5fl oz warm milk

1. Prepare the pudding basin and put a saucepan of water on to boil (see p. 74).
2. Mix all the ingredients together, adding the milk last.
3. Transfer the mixture to the pudding basin, and cover as described on p. 75.
4. Place a lid on the saucepan and steam for about four hours. (I know this is a lot longer than normal, but it is worth it.)
5. Eat with custard.

Variations
Increase the amount of dried fruit to taste. Indeed, doubling the quantities of dried fruit and adding a couple of tablespoons of black treacle will make half-pay pudding.

Marmalade Pudding

Enough for about eight.

You do not have to be a marmalade fan to like this pudding, although it does help. Do not be put off by the very large quantity of marmalade. The normal astringency of marmalade is greatly reduced by having it distributed throughout a large and solid pudding and then cooked. The recipe is derived from Mrs Beeton, and is very simple: mix together eight of everything and steam till done.

225g/8oz fresh white breadcrumbs
225g/8oz suet
225g/8oz marmalade

225g/8oz light muscovado sugar
8 eggs, lightly beaten

1. Prepare the pudding basin and put a saucepan of water on to boil (see p. 74).
2. Mix all the ingredients together, adding the eggs last.
3. Transfer the mixture to the pudding basin, and cover as described on p. 75.
4. Place a lid on the saucepan and steam for about three hours.
5. Remove the basin from the saucepan and, if desired, turn out after a few minutes. This pudding can be difficult to turn out.
6. Eat with custard.
7. Have a nap to recover from a full stomach.

Variations

Try all or any of these variations, in any combination that takes your fancy.

• *Baking powder* ~ Adding a teaspoon of baking powder makes the pudding rather lighter.

• *Butter* ~ For a lighter pudding, replace the suet with butter. If you are using butter and flour, you will need to cream the two together before folding in the remaining ingredients.

• *Custard* ~ One enticing idea, from the Three Chimneys Restaurant on the Isle of Skye, is to add a few tablespoons of Drambuie to the custard. They use brown breadcrumbs instead of white, replace some of the breadcrumbs with self-raising wholemeal flour, use butter instead of suet, halve the eggs, and add 1 tsp bicarbonate of soda mixed with 1 tsp water.

• *Eggs* ~ Half the number of eggs will in fact do fine.

• *Flour* ~ Try white or wholemeal self-raising flour instead of the breadcrumbs, or half and half flour and breadcrumbs.

• *Fruit* ~ Add the grated zest and juice of a lemon and orange.

• *Marmalade* ~ Different types of marmalade will, of course, give a different result. I think marmalade made from Seville oranges is probably best. All the books instruct one to use good-quality marmalade, and I have been too terrified ever to use any of the nasty, cheap stuff.

• *Marmalade topping* ~ You could just have the marmalade as a topping by putting it at the bottom of the basin, rather than throughout the pudding.

• *Sugar* ~ Caster or light brown sugar is fine; I think light muscovado is a particularly good idea.

• *Syrup* ~ Replace some of the sugar with some golden syrup.

• *Whisky* ~ Add a few tablespoons to the mixture.

Snowdon Pudding

This will feed about eight.

This pudding is named after the Welsh mountain, and it is said it was made for Victorian mountaineers. It is particularly appropriate in March if Wales have won the rugby, which does happen just occasionally. I tend to eat it with custard, but traditionally it is eaten with white sauce, which when poured over the pudding looks a bit like snow (see below for recipe). Do not be put off if you do not like marmalade much; as with most marmalade puddings, the taste is very much ameliorated in the cooking and by the other ingredients.

225g/8oz fresh white breadcrumbs
60g/2oz cornflour
225g/8oz suet
115g/4oz sultanas
115g/4oz white sugar
150ml/5fl oz milk

Finely grated zest of two lemons and
  the juice of one lemon
140g/5oz lemon marmalade
Pinch of salt
3 eggs, lightly beaten

1. Prepare the pudding bowl (see p. 74). It is a good idea to put a circle of greaseproof paper in the bottom to stop the pudding from sticking.
2. Put a large saucepan of water on to boil.
3. Mix all the ingredients together, adding the eggs last.
4. Transfer the mixture to the pudding basin, and cover as described on p. 75.
5. Place a lid on the saucepan and steam for about three hours.
6. Eat with custard.

Variations

• *Cherries* ~ Put some glacé cherries and raisins on the bottom of the basin to give it some colour.

• *Eggs* ~ Add five eggs instead of three.

• *Marmalade* ~ Use ordinary marmalade instead of lemon marmalade, or perhaps apricot jam.

• *Raisins* ~ Try raisins instead of sultanas.

• *Rice* ~ Replace the cornflour with the same amount of ground rice.

• *Sugar* ~ Replace the white sugar with light brown or light muscovado.

• *Suet* ~ Halve the quantity of suet, or add a few more eggs.

• *White sauce* ~ Dissolve 2 tbsp cornflour in 600ml/1 pint milk, bring to the boil and cook for a short time (you can do this in the microwave, stirring every now and then). Then mix in 60g/2oz sugar, 25g/1oz melted butter and 1 tsp vanilla extract until thoroughly combined. Serve.

Sussex Pond Pudding

The ingredients given below are enough for eight in theory, but I don't think it really feeds more than four hungry people.

This is one of the most delightful suet puddings, and it really must be tried. It has a rich yellow sauce in the middle when cut open, which gives the pudding its name.

225g/8oz self-raising flour
115g/4oz suet
150ml/5fl oz water or milk
115g/4oz light muscovado sugar

115g/4oz butter, diced into a dozen pieces
1 large lemon, preferably thin-skinned

1. Prepare the pudding basin and put a saucepan of water on to boil (see p. 74).
2. Mix the flour, suet and water or milk into a dough. I find it is easiest to do this by hand.
3. Take about two-thirds of the dough and line the bottom and sides of the basin, so that there is a well in which to put the other ingredients (see below). I tend to do this by hand, which is necessary if your dough is sticky, and more fun. Or you can roll it out.
4. Take half the sugar and half of the diced butter and place it in the well. Pierce the lemon several times with a knife or skewer to allow the lemon juice to

seep out in the cooking, and place it on top of the butter and sugar. Then add the remaining diced butter and sugar.

5. Flatten the remaining dough and place on top, sealing with the existing dough at the edges. If it won't seal, brush the edges with water.
6. Cover the bowl as described on p. 75. Place in the saucepan and cover and steam for about three hours.
7. Remove from the saucepan and turn out. Give each person some of the lemon along with their portion of pudding.
8. Eat, preferably with custard, or cream if you must.

Variations

• *Cut lemons* ~ Cut the lemon into pieces, which is somewhat inauthentic but allows the lemon to seep into the pudding better.

• *No lemons* ~ Some say that the addition of the lemon is a late invention and should be omitted. I think this is silly, as it is the lemon that makes this pudding. I have seen some grated lemon rind recommended instead, which is perhaps a compromise. The lemon is quite pronounced, and there is some sense in reducing the quantity.

• *Limes* ~ Replace the lemon with a couple of limes. This has bite, but is for grown-ups rather than children.

• *Sugar* ~ Try light soft brown, demerara or dark brown sugar instead of the light muscovado.

• *Larger quantities* ~ In principle, I prefer double quantities for steamed puddings, but it doesn't work well for this pudding. You could make two separate ones at the same time. One and a half quantities does work; increase the cooking time by 15 minutes or so.

• *Kentish Well pudding* ~ This variation uses an alternative filling of the juice and rind of a lemon (or continue to use a whole lemon), a tablespoon of golden syrup (optional), a peeled, cored and chopped Bramley apple (optional), about 115g/4oz of currants, raisins or sultanas or a mixture of them (which can be added to the suet mixture instead), along, of course, with the butter and sugar.

Steamed Sponge Puddings

While I put these in alphabetical order, I cannot emphasise too strongly that ginger and syrup steamed sponge pudding is the best in the world, although I would concede that steamed sticky toffee pudding and perhaps one or two others run it a close second.

The basic ingredients are about 225g/8oz each of self-raising flour, sugar and butter, with a few eggs (traditionally the same weight; four eggs weigh about 225g/8oz). Most books give you half these quantities, but that is barely worth making, in my view. My quantities should feed eight people, perhaps six if they have a reasonably healthy appetite. You might think each pudding should go further, but I never seem to have any left after seconds.

The only technical issue to be addressed is how to make a steamed pudding light rather than solid, assuming that is what you want to do. This may be a problem, particularly if you are adding a lot of ingredients in addition to flour, sugar, butter and eggs. There are four basic ways of doing this, and you can use any combination you like.

• Sift the flour, which will ensure that it is well aerated.
• If you just throw all the ingredients into the food processor together, this will produce a heavier pudding. Instead, cream the sugar and butter, add the eggs and any dried fruit or whatever, and then fold in the flour, i.e. add it in quite gently, preferably by hand.
• Use more flour, rather than equal quantities with the butter and sugar.
• Add up to 1 tsp baking powder to the self-raising flour.

Basic Steamed Sponge Pudding

Will feed six to eight people.

I will set out how to make a steamed sponge pudding, and then repeat the method in summary only for each recipe. Needless to say, no one ever makes a pudding without adding some flavouring, but this will give the basic structure.

225g/8oz white or brown sugar
225g/8oz cold butter
4 eggs

225g/8oz self-raising flour
About 2 tbsp milk

1. Prepare the pudding basin and put a saucepan of water on to boil (see p. 74).
2. Put the sugar and butter (cut up into a dozen or so pieces) into a food processor and whizz to a nice paste.
3. Beat the eggs together lightly with a fork. Add them to the food processor with a little of the flour and process for a couple of quick blasts.
4. Add the rest of the flour and whizz in. Do not process for more than necessary to mix the ingredients together. This should not take too long.
5. The mixture should be reasonably solid rather than liquid, but not too stiff. If it is too stiff, add a couple of tablespoons of milk and whizz in.
6. Spoon the mixture into the buttered pudding basin. It should not come much more than halfway up the bowl, as there needs to be room for expansion.
7. Cover the pudding basin as described on p. 75, place in the saucepan of boiling water and cook for about two hours or so, testing to see whether it is done a couple of times in the last half hour.
8. Remove from the saucepan and decant from the bowl (optional).
9. Serve with proper homemade custard.

Variation in method
I am a bit finickity about creaming the butter and sugar together, and then adding the other ingredients. One can simply put all the ingredients into a food processor and blitz them together. I cannot honestly say that the results are measurably worse. However, the problem with doing it this way is that there is less air in the mixture, so you will need to add up to 1 tsp baking powder to the mixture, or increase the quantities of flour slightly.

Black Cap Pudding

Serves eight people.

A straightforward and tasty steamed pudding.

115g/4oz raisins or currants or
  6 tbsp blackcurrant jam
225g/8oz butter
115g/4oz caster sugar

6 eggs
225g/8oz self-raising flour
Finely grated zest of a lemon (optional)
About 2 tbsp milk

1. Prepare the pudding basin and put a saucepan of water on to boil (see p. 74).
2. Put the currants, raisins or blackcurrant jam in the pudding basin.
3. Cream the butter and sugar.
4. Beat the eggs and mix them gently into the butter and sugar mixture.
5. Add the flour to the mixture, folding it in gently, and then the lemon zest.
6. The mixture should be reasonably solid rather than liquid, but not too stiff. If too stiff, add 1–2 tbsp milk and mix in.
7. Spoon the mixture into the pudding basin, on top of the dried fruit or jam.
8. Cover the basin as described on p. 75, place in the pan of boiling water and cook for about two hours.
9. Serve with real custard.

Canary Pudding

Serves about eight people.

First take two canaries. Actually, don't. The name comes from the yellow colour of the pudding, rather than the use of canaries in making it – not that it is much yellower than any other sponge pudding, really. There are, of course, a number of different recipes for this. I think that the most important ingredient is probably the jam sauce.

For the sponge:
225g/8oz caster sugar
225g/8oz butter
6 eggs
225g/8oz self-raising flour
Finely grated zest of a lemon
About 2 tbsp milk

For the jam sauce:
2 tsp cornflour
300ml/10fl oz water
4 tbsp jam
2 tbsp sugar
Juice of half a lemon (optional)

1. Prepare the pudding basin and put a saucepan of water on to boil (see p. 74).
2. Cream the butter and sugar.
3. Beat the eggs and mix them gently into the butter and sugar mixture.
4. Add the flour to the mixture, folding it in gently, and then the grated lemon zest. The mixture should be reasonably solid rather than liquid, but not too stiff. If it is too stiff, add a few tablespoons of milk.

5. Spoon the mixture into the pudding basin, and cover as described on p. 75.

6. Place in the saucepan of boiling water and cook for about two hours.

7. Make the jam sauce. Dissolve the cornflour in the cold water, making sure all the lumps have disappeared. Pour this and the remaining sauce ingredients into a saucepan and bring to the boil, stirring until thickened, which will only be a couple of minutes.

8. Serve the pudding with proper custard as well as the jam sauce.

Variations

• *Breadcrumbs* ~ Replace half of the flour with breadcrumbs.

• *Eggs* ~ Mrs Beeton halves the number of eggs.

• *Lemon juice* ~ Add the juice of half a lemon instead of the zest.

• *Orange zest* ~ Use instead of lemon zest.

• *Sherry* ~ Add a few tablespoons of sweet sherry to the mixture; stir it in with the eggs.

• *Suet* ~ Replace the butter with suet for a heavier pudding.

• *Vanilla* ~ Try a teaspoon of vanilla extract instead of the lemon zest.

• *Other variations* ~ Try adding sultanas, candied peel, glacé ginger, or glacé cherries.

Chocolate Pudding

This is for up to eight people.

There are very few people who do not like chocolate pudding. It is, of course, much like chocolate cake, but rather better I think. If you are running out of time, you can bake this pudding instead for 45–60 minutes at 400F/200C/gas mark 6, or try baked chocolate surprise pudding (p. 106) or microwave chocolate pudding (p. 158). As always, if you want to make a more normal-sized pudding, halve the quantities and cook for about half an hour less, or for a bigger one double the quantities and cook for around half an hour more. It is best eaten with chocolate sauce; my favourite recipe for this is set out below.

225g/8oz butter
225g/8oz soft brown or caster sugar
4 eggs

1 tsp vanilla extract (optional)
225g/8oz self-raising flour
3–4 tbsp of cocoa powder, sifted

1. Prepare the pudding basin and put a saucepan of water on to boil (see p. 74).
2. Cream the butter and sugar.
3. Beat the eggs, add them to the butter and sugar mixture and lightly mix in. Add the vanilla extract, if using.
4. Add the flour and cocoa to the mixture, folding them in gently.
5. Spoon the mixture into the pudding basin, and cover as described on p. 75.
6. Place in the saucepan of boiling water, cover, and cook for about two hours.
7. Serve the pudding with custard, chocolate custard (see p. 27) or chocolate sauce (see below). If you are really greedy, do both.

Chocolate sauce
You can use a bain-marie or double boiler for any of these sauces, although I don't bother. Cook them on the hob, or try making them in the microwave instead.

• *A good chocolate sauce* ~ For a good dark chocolate sauce, take 300ml/10fl oz double cream, 170g/6oz butter, 60g/2oz sugar (preferably light muscovado), 170g/6oz dark chocolate, and 1 tsp vanilla extract (optional). Break the chocolate into pieces, put all the ingredients in a saucepan, and gently heat for about five minutes until melted together and hot, stirring occasionally. This can be done in the microwave instead. I think that this sauce is fantastic, and normally make double quantities.

• *Milk chocolate* ~ Children are unlikely to be keen on a dark chocolate sauce, so try milk chocolate instead.

• *A lighter sauce* ~ Make a less rich chocolate sauce by omitting the cream and reducing the butter to about 60g/2oz, adding a few tablespoons of water; in other words a total of 60g/2oz butter, 60g/2oz sugar, 170g/6oz dark chocolate, 1 tsp vanilla extract (optional), and some water.

• *Chocolate and orange sauce* ~ To make a chocolate and orange sauce, add the zest and juice of an orange to any dark chocolate sauce.

• *White chocolate sauce* ~ Take 225g/8oz white chocolate, broken into pieces, and 150ml/5fl oz double cream. Melt the ingredients together on a gentle heat, stirring until melted. A couple of tablespoons of brandy or Amaretto can be added.

Variations
• *Banana and chocolate puddings* ~ Mash about three ripe bananas in a bowl and stir them into the creamed butter and sugar before adding the other ingredients.

• *Breadcrumbs* ~ Use these instead of flour.

• *Chocolate* ~ Replace the cocoa with 85g/3oz melted chocolate.

• *Chocolate topping* ~ You can give the pudding a chocolate topping by putting some chocolate in the pudding bowl before adding the sponge mixture. Try 170g/6oz chocolate chips. Or take up to 350g/12oz plain chocolate in pieces, 150ml/5fl oz double cream and 4 tbsp caster sugar, and gently melt together before putting in the bottom.

• *Cocoa* ~ The amount of cocoa powder will depend on how chocolatey you want the pudding. Children may not like it too strong.

• *Orange* ~ This, of course, goes well with chocolate. Add, for instance, the grated zest of an orange and half of the juice as well. An alternative is to take an orange, boil it for 10 minutes, prick it all over when cooled, and put in the middle of the mixture before cooking; half quantities of the pudding are probably better for this.

• *Suet* ~ Use instead of butter to make a heavier pudding.

Ginger and Syrup Pudding

This makes a reasonably substantial pudding for up to eight people.

While there are some steamed puddings that are even simpler and quicker to make, this one is not difficult. It is wonderful. This is what the gods eat. You can make half quantities, but I find that however much I make, and however few people there are to eat it, this pudding all goes, and it is advisable to have a second lighter pudding in reserve.

For the topping:
300ml/10fl oz golden syrup
2.5cm/1in stem ginger, peeled and
  chopped quite finely
For the sponge:
225g/8oz self-raising flour

2 tsp ground ginger
225g/8oz soft brown or caster sugar
225g/8oz butter
4 eggs
About 2 tbsp milk

1. Prepare the pudding basin, and put a saucepan of water on to boil (see p. 74).
2. Put a 1cm/½in layer of golden syrup in the bottom of the basin. This is sticky work. You can make it easier by heating the syrup first.
3. Stir the chopped ginger into the syrup.
4. Mix the flour and ground ginger together in another bowl.
5. Cream the sugar and butter in a food processor.
6. Beat the eggs, add to the food processor and mix for a couple of quick blasts.
7. Add the flour and ginger to the processor and whizz in. Do not process for more than necessary to mix the ingredients together.
8. The mixture should be reasonably solid rather than liquid, but not too stiff. If too stiff, add a few tablespoons of milk and whizz in.
9. Spoon the mixture into the pudding bowl. For this pudding, you will have to try to keep the mixture on top of the syrup. If the syrup comes up the sides a bit, do not worry; sometimes the mixture looks like an iceberg swimming in an oil slick. Smooth off the top of the mixture, rather than leaving it in lumps.
10. Cover the pudding bowl as described on p. 75, place in the pan of boiling water, and cook for about two hours.
11. If you decant the pudding from the bowl on to a plate, make sure it is a very big plate, otherwise the syrup will overflow.
12. Serve with real custard. This pudding deserves a proper pudding wine.

Some variations
• *Black treacle* ~ Replace 1 tbsp or so of the golden syrup with black treacle. Or use the black treacle in place of about 15g/1oz of the sugar in the sponge.

• *No ginger* ~ Omit the ginger for a plain, steamed treacle sponge. In this case, I like to add the grated rind of a lemon to the sponge mixture. If you like it very lemony, juice the lemon as well and add half the juice to the sponge mixture and stir the other half into the golden syrup.

Lemon Pudding

Serves six to eight people.

225g/8oz lemon curd (a purist will
  make his own, I don't)
225g/8oz butter
225g/8oz caster sugar

6 eggs
Finely grated zest of 2 lemons
225g/8oz self-raising flour
About 2 tbsp milk

1. Prepare the pudding basin, and put a saucepan of water on to boil (see p. 74).
2. Spoon the lemon curd into the base of the pudding basin.
3. Cream the butter and sugar.
4. Beat the eggs, add them with the lemon rind to the butter and sugar mixture and lightly mix in.
5. Add the flour to the mixture, folding it in gently.
6. The mixture should be reasonably solid rather than liquid, but not too stiff. If too stiff, add a few tablespoons of milk and whizz in.
7. Spoon the mixture into the pudding basin.
8. Cover the basin as described on p. 75, place in the pan of boiling water, and cook for about two hours.
9. Serve the pudding with proper egg custard. I like using lemon custard (see p. 28).

Variations
• *Orange* ~ Use orange curd and the grated zest of an orange instead of lemon.

• *Uncooked lemon curd* ~ Add the lemon curd after the pudding has been cooked and turned out.

Plum Jam Pudding

Serves six to eight people.

The difference between this jam pudding and most others is the addition of almonds, an idea I found in *The Pudding Club Book* (although they use far too much flour for my liking). This creates a distinctive flavour in the sponge, which nicely sets off the jam. The addition of the ground almonds makes the pudding a little heavier than most steamed puddings, hence the addition of a teaspoon of baking powder.

225g/8oz plum jam (this sounds a lot, but it is worthwhile)
225g/8oz butter
225g/8oz caster sugar
4–6 eggs

170g/6oz self-raising flour
1 tsp baking powder
60g/2oz ground almonds
1 tsp almond extract (optional)

1. Prepare the pudding basin and put a saucepan of water on to boil (see p. 74).
2. Put the jam into the bottom of the pudding basin.
3. Cream the butter and sugar.
4. Beat the eggs, then add them to the butter and sugar mixture and lightly mix them in.
5. Mix the flour with the baking powder and add it to the mixture along with the ground almonds, folding it in gently if possible. Add the almond extract, if using.
6. Spoon the mixture into the pudding basin on top of the jam.
7. Cover the basin as described on p. 75, place in boiling water and cook for about two hours.
8. Serve the pudding with real custard.

Variations
• *No almonds* ~ If omitting the almonds, add 60g/2oz self-raising flour.

• *Lemon juice* ~ Try adding a couple of tablespoons of lemon juice to the jam.

• *Jam* ~ Try any other jam that goes well with almonds.

• *Marmalade* ~ Replace the jam with marmalade.

• *St Clement's pudding* ~ Replace the jam with 170g/6oz orange marmalade (omitted in some recipes), and add the juice and grated zest of a couple of oranges to the sponge.

Rhubarb Pudding

Serves six to eight.

As a rhubarb lover, I could hardly miss out a rhubarb steamed pudding. This is a relatively moist and dense pudding. No additional liquid should be added, as rhubarb produces quite a lot of juice, which gets absorbed into the pudding.

450g/1lb rhubarb	225g/8oz self-raising flour
225g/8oz butter	1 tsp baking powder
285g/10oz caster or soft brown sugar	2 tsp ground ginger
4 eggs	

1. Prepare the pudding basin and put a saucepan of water on to boil (see p. 74).
2. Cut the rhubarb up into small pieces. I think it is best to split any big pieces lengthways once or twice, and then cut the rhubarb up into thin pieces about ½cm/¼in or so long.
3. Cream the butter and sugar.
4. Beat the eggs, then add them to the butter and sugar mixture and lightly mix them in.
5. Add the flour, baking powder and ground ginger to the mixture, folding them in gently.
6. Gently fold in the rhubarb.
7. Spoon the mixture into the pudding bowl. Cover the bowl as described on p. 75, place in the pan of boiling water and cook for about two and a half or three hours; I think this pudding seems to need a bit longer than most steamed puddings.
8. Eat with custard.

Sticky Toffee Pudding

Sufficient for about eight.

This date-filled sponge pudding with butterscotch sauce was invented by Francis Coulson, who ran what now would be called a country house hotel soon after the Second World War. It is deservedly popular. There are any number of variations for this, but in my opinion none of the other recipes I have seen makes nearly enough sauce. I have doubled the normal quantity here, and it almost always gets eaten as quickly as the pudding. I have a friend who quadruples the normal quantities, and keeps any left in jars as a topping for ice cream and the like. Being mean with the sauce is hopeless. This pudding is traditionally baked, but I much prefer it steamed, which is why it is in this chapter and not Chapter 9.

For the pudding:	½ tsp vanilla extract
225g/8oz dates	For the sauce:
1 tsp bicarbonate of soda	450g/1lb light muscovado sugar
115g/4oz butter	300ml/10fl oz double cream
170g/6oz light muscovado sugar	225g/8oz butter
3 eggs, lightly beaten	1 tsp vanilla extract
225g/8oz self-raising flour	

1. Prepare the pudding basin and put a saucepan of water on to boil (see p. 74).
2. Stone and chop the dates and put them in a saucepan on the stove. Pour on 300ml/10fl oz boiling water and bring to the boil. Remove from the stove and stir in the bicarbonate of soda, which will bubble up. Leave to cool for a few minutes.
3. Cream the butter and sugar, add the eggs, fold in the flour, then add the dates and their liquid and the vanilla extract.
4. Transfer to the pudding bowl, cover as described on p. 75, place in boiling water, and cook for about two hours.
5. Make the sauce. This can be done while the pudding is steaming. Just mix all the ingredients together, bring to the boil, and simmer gently until melted and smooth. Give it a stir very occasionally.
6. Take the pudding out of the basin. Pour some of the sauce over the pudding and leave to soak in for 10 minutes.

7. Serve with the rest of the sticky toffee sauce, and also with ice cream, cream, custard or crème fraîche, if wanted.

Variations

• *Method* ~ Instead of cooking the sauce separately, a 'surprise' pudding can be made. The sugar and butter should be sprinkled over the top of the pudding before cooking, the cream omitted, and 900ml/1½ pints of boiling water poured over the top. The sauce ends up at the bottom of the pudding.

• *Baked* ~ This pudding can be baked instead; pour the mixture into a buttered bowl or baking tin and bake for 30–40 minutes at 350F/180C/gas mark 4.

• *Golden syrup* ~ Add a couple of tablespoons of golden syrup to the sauce, reducing the sugar by 25–60g/1–2oz. Or try a tablespoon or two of black treacle, or a tablespoon or less of lemon juice.

• *Sugar* ~ Replace the sugar in the pudding, or in the sauce, or both, with caster, light brown, demerara, light or dark muscovado. I prefer light muscovado, but only for the sauce.

• *Walnuts* ~ Replace the dates with chopped walnuts, or omit altogether.

Breadcrumb Steamed Puddings

There are some steamed puddings involving breadcrumbs in the steamed suet section above. Here are a few that normally don't use suet. They are, of course, pretty interchangeable.

Bachelor's Pudding

Serves eight.

I think the name is derived from the fact that lonely bachelors can cook this simple pudding and consume it on their own. But having tried that once, they are likely to want to keep the pudding to themselves and therefore stay single. This recipe is pretty well straight from Mrs Beeton, although

I have doubled the quantities. It is ridiculously easy to make; the only thing that requires a bit of effort is preparing the apples. It is jolly good, yet I have never yet come across anyone else who has even eaten it (save at my table), let alone made it. What is most unusual about it is the absence of any butter.

225g/8oz fresh white breadcrumbs	115g/4oz caster sugar
225g/8oz currants	6 eggs, separated
225g/8oz apples, peeled, cored and grated	Finely grated zest of a lemon
	A whole grated nutmeg (or try less)

1. Prepare the pudding basin and put a saucepan of water on to boil (see p. 74).
2. Mix all the ingredients together.
3. Put the mixture in the pudding basin and cover as described on p. 75.
4. Steam for three and a half hours (three if using half quantities).
5. Eat with custard, of course.

Guard's Pudding

Feeds eight.

This is a straightforward steamed pudding with a jam base.

225g/8oz butter	2 eggs
225g/8oz soft brown sugar	1 tsp bicarbonate of soda
225g/8oz fresh white breadcrumbs	6 tbsp raspberry or strawberry jam

1. Prepare the pudding basin and put a saucepan of water on to boil (see p. 74).
2. Cream the butter and sugar together in a food processor.
3. Add the remaining ingredients and whizz together.
4. Put the ingredients in a pudding basin and cover as described on p. 75.
5. Place in the pan of boiling water and steam for three hours.
6. Eat with custard.

Variations
Use suet instead of butter (in which case just combine all the ingredients together), or flour instead of breadcrumbs, or brown breadcrumbs.

Prince Albert Pudding

Feeds eight.

There are relatively few proper prune puddings about. This is perhaps the best. I will set out the quantity for a large pudding; you can halve the amounts and reduce the cooking time to about two hours, if you really want to. This pudding is a little more complicated to make than many, but it is worth the hassle. The prunes need to be soaked in advance, so you cannot decide to make this pudding at only three hours' notice. The egg whites do need to be whisked and then folded into the mixture, which requires a very little bit of skill, but nothing approaching what is needed for a soufflé. And you need a lot of little bowls to put all the bits and pieces in.

450g/1lb prunes
350g/12oz butter
225g/8oz caster sugar
6 eggs

285g/10oz breadcrumbs, white
  or brown
Grated zest of 2 lemons
About 450ml/15fl oz milk

1. Soak the prunes in about 600ml/1 pint water. It is best to do this overnight, but you can speed it up by slicing the prunes in two and soaking them in boiling water.
2. Prepare the pudding basin (see p. 74). Place a circle of baking parchment at the bottom of the bowl to make it easier to get the pudding out after cooking.
3. Put a saucepan of water on to boil.
4. Drain the prunes.
5. Melt a third of the butter by cutting it into pieces and heating it for 10 or 20 seconds in the microwave. Mix the melted butter in with the prunes. Press the prunes evenly against the bottom and sides of the basin. This is a good task for a small child.
6. Cream the remaining (still cold) butter with the sugar.
7. Separate the eggs. Fold the egg yolks, breadcrumbs and lemon rind into the butter and sugar mixture.
8. Then add the milk a bit at a time until the mixture is a soft, dropping consistency.
9. Whisk the egg whites until they are white and stiff enough to form little peaks. Make sure that they are not too beaten, or the peaks will be too stiff.

10. Gently fold the egg whites into the mixture, using a large metal spoon.
11. Transfer the mixture to the basin, trying not to disturb the prune 'casing'.
12. Cover as described on p. 75 and steam for three hours.
13. Eat with custard.

Variations
• *Alcohol* ~ The addition of few tablespoons of sherry or brandy is nice.

• *Ground rice* ~ Replace about a third of the breadcrumbs with ground rice.

CHAPTER 9
Baked
Puddings

I SUPPOSE the title of this chapter is a bit misleading, because crumbles, milk puddings, bread and butter pudding, tarts and pies are all baked, of course. I refer, though, to suet, sponge or breadcrumb puddings that are baked, which are the equivalent of the steamed puddings in the previous chapter. They are quicker to cook than steamed puddings and slightly easier to make, as you don't have to cover them so elaborately before cooking them. On the other hand, they are not quite so easy-going when it comes to cooking times, and you can burn them. Any steamed pudding can be baked, of course, or vice versa, but this chapter is made up of puddings that I think are much better if baked, which includes a classic chocolate surprise pudding and queen of puddings, which has been undeservedly forgotten.

Chocolate Surprise Pudding

This should be enough for eight people.

The surprise is that the chocolate sauce mixture, which is on the top of the pudding before baking, ends up on the bottom, with the pudding getting gradually thicker and crispier as you head up to the top. This recipe is an adaptation of the recipe used by the Pudding Club. You can halve the quantity if you want a smallish pudding. It is a rich, dark pudding, not ideally suitable for children (unless you use at least some milk chocolate). It really needs a large wide dish, or you can use two of a more ordinary size.

For the base:
115g/4oz dark chocolate
85g/3oz butter, cut into half a dozen
  pieces
300ml/10 fl oz milk, warmed
350g/12oz sugar (yes, really)
225g/8oz plain flour
4 tsp baking powder

2 tsp vanilla extract (optional)
2 eggs (optional)
For the sauce:
285g/10oz sugar: either light brown
  or a mixture of white and dark brown
  or light muscovado
4 tbsp cocoa powder
600ml/1 pint hot water

1. Heat the oven to 325F/160C/gas mark 3.
2. Break the chocolate into pieces and melt it either in the microwave in a biggish bowl, 10 or 20 seconds at a time, or in a pan over a low heat.

3. When the chocolate is nearly melted, add the butter and melt it into the chocolate.
4. Add and mix in the warmed milk.
5. Add the sugar, flour, baking powder and vanilla extract and mix in well. Beat in the eggs.
6. Transfer to the baking dish. Scatter the additional sugar and cocoa powder evenly over the top of the pudding and pour the water into the dish. I prefer to have hot or boiling water, but this is not essential.
7. Cook in the oven for about an hour.
8. Serve on its own, or with cream or chocolate custard (see p. 27).

Eve's Pudding

This will feed four or so, six at a pinch.

This pudding is supposedly so named because of the tempting apples beneath the sponge. I normally double the quantities, which needs an hour's cooking. It is good with custard. I confess that I find ordinary unadulterated Eve's pudding a little dull, but the variations spice it up immensely.

12oz/350g cooking apples	115g/4oz caster sugar
85g/3oz light brown or caster sugar	2 eggs
For the topping:	115g/4oz self-raising flour
115g/4oz butter	½ tsp vanilla extract (optional)

1. Preheat the oven to about 350F/180C/gas mark 4, and butter a dish.
2. Peel and core the apples, and chop them up.
3. Mix the apples and brown sugar and tip them into the buttered dish.
4. Cream the butter and caster sugar.
5. Beat the eggs and mix them in with the butter and sugar.
6. Fold in the flour and vanilla extract (if using); you may need a little milk to get a soft enough consistency to spread the mixture.
7. Spread the sponge mixture over the top of the apples.
8. Bake for about 45 minutes.
9. Eat, preferably with custard, or cream.

Some variations

• *Increasing the apples* ~ The traditional quantity is 450g/1lb, which I think is a little too much.

• *Apricots* ~ Add some dried apricots, cut into small pieces, to the apples. Use about a quarter of the weight of dried apricots to apples. Some almond extract added to the sponge mixture is a good idea.

• *Baking powder* ~ Add ½ tsp baking powder to make a lighter sponge.

• *Black treacle and raisins* ~ Add 1 tbsp black treacle and 60g/2oz raisins to the apples, omitting the light brown sugar.

• *Blackberries* ~ Add some blackberries to the apples. This is a particularly good pudding. The blackberries can stand stronger sugars in the fruit and the sponge than apples alone; try light brown and dark brown respectively.

• *Lemon* ~ Add the juice of a lemon to the apple mixture, or the grated zest of a lemon to the sponge mixture along with the flour, or both.

• *Marmalade* ~ Add 2 tbsp marmalade to the apples.

• *Rhubarb* ~ Substitute rhubarb for apples, and add some ginger, or try apricots.

• *Spices* ~ Try 1 tsp ground cinnamon in the apple mixture.

• *Sultanas* ~ Add 115g/4oz sultanas, reducing the sugar by half.

Fruit Suet Crust

Serves eight people.

I think of this as an easy alternative to crumble: same fruit; slightly different topping; same cooking time. It is denser and more solid than crumble, and a good alternative once in a while. This pudding can be steamed instead (for about three hours), or boiled in a pudding bowl (for about two hours).

For the fruit:
900g/2lb rhubarb
60g/2oz sugar
1 tsp ground ginger

For the suet crust:
225g/8oz self-raising flour
115g/4oz shredded suet
85g/3oz caster sugar
Water to mix

1. Preheat the oven to about 375F/190C/gas mark 5.
2. Cut the rhubarb into small logs about 1cm/½in long.
3. Put the fruit, sugar and ginger into a reasonably deep ovenproof bowl, and stir to mix.
4. Mix the flour, suet, caster sugar and some water in a large mixing bowl. It is best to start with a moderate quantity of water (150ml/5fl oz at most), and add more if necessary. The dough should be firm.
5. Roll out the suet crust and place on top of the fruit mixture, making sure there are no gaps around the edge. (I think it is easier just to spread the crust on the pudding with your fingers.)
6. Cook for about 40 minutes, until the crust is risen and golden.
7. Eat with custard.

Variations

• *Apples* ~ Use 900g/2lb cooking apples, peeled, cored and sliced, instead of the rhubarb. This is often known as apple hat pudding. Try adding to this 60g/2oz or so of chopped dates and some lemon juice.

• *Fruit* ~ Replace the rhubarb with another fruit of your choice, such as blackcurrants, gooseberries, blackberries, a mixture of blackberries and apples, and so on. A mixture of rhubarb and plum is very good. If you use blackberries by themselves, you will only need 450g/1lb, but for all other fruits or combinations of fruit, use 900g/2lb.

• *Suet all round* ~ You can envelop the fruit entirely in suet if you prefer, in which case the crust will be rather thinner than if you just have a suet topping. Increase the quantity of ingredients for the suet crust by about half, and reduce the fruit to 675g/1½lb. Roll out the dough (or squash it out), and use it to line the bowl first, leaving about a third of the dough for the lid. Place the fruit mixture inside, and cover and seal with the dough lid.

Ipswich Almond Pudding

Will feed about four people.

This breadcrumb pudding, which is pretty well Bakewell tart without the tart, is quite simple to make. It is not large or filling, and nearly counts as a light pudding or dessert. The amount of orange water seems quite a lot, but if you are going to taste and smell this, you need quite a lot of it. To feed more than four, you can double the quantities, of course, in which case add about 15 minutes to the cooking time.

60g/2oz breadcrumbs	60g/2oz sugar
300ml/10fl oz double cream	170g/6oz ground almonds
3 egg yolks	2 tbsp orange flower water (optional)
60g/2oz butter	2 or 3 egg whites

1. Soak the breadcrumbs in the cream for at least 10 minutes.
2. Heat the oven to 325F/160C/gas mark 3, and butter a smallish dish.
3. Whisk the egg yolks lightly together. Melt the butter.
4. Combine all the ingredients except the egg whites.
5. Whisk the egg whites until stiff and fold them gently into the mixture with a metal spoon. Transfer the mixture to the buttered dish.
6. Bake the pudding for about 30–40 minutes. I like to sprinkle some sugar on top halfway through the cooking to get a nice sugary crust.
7. Serve with cream not custard.

Variations

• *Almonds* ~ I like this pudding with a lot of ground almonds. Some recipes suggest as little as a third of what I put in, which does produce a lighter pudding.

• *A heavier pudding* ~ If you miss out whisking and folding in the egg whites and just stir them in instead, you will still have a perfectly serviceable pudding, but it will be rather less light.

• *Cream* ~ You could add 300ml/10fl oz milk to the cream, a variation that appears in many recipes.

Lemon Surprise Pudding

This will feed four, but you can double the quantities and cook it in two dishes.

This is a delicious, light pudding. The surprise is that the mixture separates into a fluffy top layer and a juicy bottom layer. Don't be surprised by the small amount of flour; the egg whites act as the raising agent.

4 eggs	Grated zest and juice of 2 lemons
60g/2oz butter	60g/2oz self-raising flour
170g/6oz caster sugar	150ml/5fl oz milk

1. Heat the oven to 350F/180C/gas mark 4, and butter a large soufflé dish.
2. Separate the eggs.
3. Cream the butter and sugar.
4. Add the lemon juice and grated zest. The mixture will probably curdle, but do not worry.
5. Beat in the egg yolks, and then the flour and milk.
6. Whisk the egg whites and gently fold them into the mixture.
7. Pour into the soufflé dish and bake for 40–45 minutes until golden.
8. Serve, perhaps with cream.

Military Pudding

Serves 8

You can imagine the scene in the barracks: Soldier 1: 'Pass me the Military Pudding.' Soldier 2: 'I can't.' Soldier 1: 'Why not?' Soldier 2: 'It's against regulations to help another soldier to dessert.' This pudding is pretty well straight out of Mrs Beeton, and is just a baked suet pudding with lemon.

225g/8oz breadcrumbs	225g/8oz soft brown sugar
225g/8oz suet	Grated zest and juice of a large lemon

1. Mix all the ingredients together and bake in a baking dish for about 45 minutes at 400F/200C/gas mark 6. Serve.

Variation
You could spread the bottom of the bowl with jam, or (as Mrs Beeton recommends) cook the pudding in individual cups (castle moulds or ramekins would be better) for half an hour.

Queen of Puddings

This will feed six people.

Queen of puddings is very delicious, if somewhat sweet, and it is very surprising it is not better known. It was supposedly developed for Queen Victoria by her chefs at Buckingham Palace. However, it may have derived from Manchester pudding, which is essentially queen of puddings all baked at the same time rather than in stages, or, in some versions, without the meringue. The basic idea is to have a layer of breadcrumbs soaked in custard at the bottom, some raspberry jam or other fruit in the middle, and then a layer of meringue on top. In Mrs Beeton's recipe the pie dish is lined with puff or flaky pastry first. In Wales, queen of puddings is known as Monmouth pudding.

115–140g/4–5oz white or brown
  breadcrumbs
140g/5oz sugar
Grated zest of a large lemon
1 tsp vanilla extract (optional)

600ml/1 pint milk
60g/2oz butter
4 eggs, the yolks for the base and the
  whites for the meringue
3 tbsp raspberry jam

1. Heat the oven to 325–350F/160–180C/gas mark 3–4, and butter a pudding dish, for instance a pie dish. A clear one is a good idea, because then you can see the layers of the pudding.
2. Put the breadcrumbs, 25g/1oz of the sugar, the grated lemon zest and vanilla into a pudding basin and mix.
3. Heat the milk to below boiling point. Melt the butter.
4. Stir the milk and butter into the breadcrumb mixture and leave for at least 10 minutes
5. Separate the eggs. Mix the egg yolks into the breadcrumb mixture, but reserve the whites for the meringue.

6. Transfer the mixture to the pudding dish, and cook for about half an hour, until the custard is just firm.

7. Take the pudding out of the oven, and while cooling a little carry out the next two steps.

8. Heat the jam gently to thin it. When it is reasonably runny, spread evenly over the custard mixture.

9. Whisk the egg whites until reasonably stiff then add the remaining sugar a spoonful at a time, whisking thoroughly after each addition.

10. Pile the meringue on top of the pudding, and sprinkle a teaspoon of sugar over the top.

11. Return to the oven for about 25 minutes, until the meringue is slightly brown.

12. Eat hot, warm or cold, on its own or with cream or crème fraîche.

Cooking tips

• *Bread* ~ If you are feeling too lazy to make breadcrumbs, then cut the crusts off the bread, roughly cube it, soak it in the hot milk for at least 15 minutes, and whisk into a purée when the bread is soft enough.

• *Cooking in one go* ~ You can assemble the pudding and cook it all in one go. The meringue will be rather firmer. The difficulty is spreading the jam and meringue on a less stable base.

• *Heating the jam* ~ I think the easiest way to do this is in the microwave, but be careful with the hot jam, as it burns if it is too hot. It should be runny enough to pour and spread over the pudding without breaking the surface. The surface is less likely to break if the pudding has cooled down for a few minutes.

• *Heating the milk and butter* ~ I think the simplest way to do this is to heat the milk in the microwave for about three minutes. Then put the butter in the microwave, cut up into bits, and blast for about half a minute or so, 10 seconds at a time. You could also add the cut up bits of butter to the milk before heating, and stir once it is hot.

• *Jam on the bottom* ~ Instead of spreading the jam on the hot pudding, you can put the jam on the bottom of the pie dish and spread it evenly before pouring the custardy breadcrumb mixture over the top.

Variations

All quantities are somewhat approximate and can be varied according to taste. For instance, if you want the pudding less rich, you can reduce or omit the butter, or reduce the number of eggs to, say, three. You can also reduce the sugar by up to a half; the pudding is already pretty sweet.

• *Almonds* ~ These can be added in a variety of ways. I like putting ½ tsp almond extract in the breadcrumb mixture, and adding 25–60g/1–2oz of ground almonds, too, reducing the amount of breadcrumbs by the same amount. On the top of the meringue you can sprinkle some ground almonds before cooking (but watch carefully, as they burn more easily than just the meringue), or try flaked almonds. Alternatively, use ground hazelnuts in the pudding, and whole hazelnuts on top. You can put ground nuts in the meringue, but there is a danger that it will rise less well.

• *Brandy* ~ Add about 4 tbsp brandy to the milk or egg yolks, mixing well, before adding to the breadcrumbs.

• *Chocolate* ~ Add 60g/2oz grated chocolate to the milk before it is heated. Omit the grated lemon zest. Apricot jam is better for the middle layer than raspberry if you are doing this.

• *Filling* ~ The traditional filling is raspberry jam. If you want, you can mix in 2 tsp lemon juice, which also helps make the jam runnier. However, any jam, conserve or jelly can be used. Even marmalade is possible, perhaps with 1–2 tsp golden syrup mixed in. Alternatively, use fruit purée, somewhere between 170g/6oz and 450g/1lb fruit, such as tinned or stewed fresh apricots. Or use the same quantities of any available fruit, such as apples, apricots, blackberries, blackcurrants, peaches, plums, raspberries, or whatever. Raspberries and blackberries don't need to be cooked; the other fruits will need a little cooking first.

• *Oranges* ~ You can replace the lemon zest with the grated zest of an orange.

• *Topping* ~ You can decorate the meringue before it is cooked with glacé cherries or a crown of flaked almonds.

• *Mrs Beeton's Manchester pudding* ~ Mix the hot milk (300ml/10fl oz), grated zest of half a lemon (you can instead use peel, leave it to infuse in the milk for a while, and then extract the peel), breadcrumbs (85g/3oz), about two eggs and two egg yolks, 60g/2oz sugar (or to taste), and 3 tbsp brandy. Leave to soak for at least 10 minutes. Meanwhile, line the pie dish with about 225g/8oz puff or flaky pastry (i.e. pastry based on 225g/8oz flour). Put the jam on top of the pastry, then add the custardy breadcrumb mixture and cook for about an hour at 325F/160C/gas mark 3. Mrs Beeton suggests the pudding should be eaten cold, with sugar sprinkled on top.

CHAPTER 10
Tarts

I CAME LATE to tarts. I was put off for years because they seemed to involve proper, technical cooking, unlike a crumble or a steamed pudding, which you just roughly mix up and slap together. As Mrs Beeton wrote: 'Although from Puddings to Pastry is but a step, it requires a higher degree of art to make the one than to make the other.' But then I spent one summer holiday some years ago making a lot of them, and discovered that once you master the pastry, it's not so hard.

A little practice helps a lot, and I do mean a little: if the first one doesn't come out right, then the second one should be serviceably edible, and the third or fourth acceptably elegant. I remember getting so blasé about how easy tarts were that on about the fourth one I made, I slopped too much water in without paying attention. The solution, I felt, was to add more flour and butter, and then more flour and butter. The glutinous mass did not get much better, and I was starting to feel like Paddington Bear in the kitchen, if you recall his adventure with the dumplings, because it was not easy to get rid of the very large sticky mess that was attached to the whizzer, the counter, various implements and my hands. But after a couple of blocks of butter and a mountain of flour had been wasted, and after a bit of cleaning, I started again with more success.

Perhaps the greatest advantage of tarts for a pudding maker is that they are acceptable to those who don't really like proper puddings. Furthermore, once you can make the pastry case, there are a great variety of fillings you can add, and most of them are pretty easy to do. As a result, I did get somewhat carried away in the number of recipes that I set out, as you will see. And of course, once you can make a tart, there are hundreds of savoury fillings you can put in them as well.

How to cheat
You can cheat in three ways when making tarts. First, you can buy the pastry. Secondly, you can buy a tart casing and make the filling. Thirdly, you can buy the whole pie or tart and make your own custard. Personally, I think that bought pastry does not have the same taste as any you can make yourself, and takes much of the fun out of cooking. If it is the rolling that puts you off tarts, there are some alternatives, which I set out below.

A few starting tips
There are a few things to know about pastry, which, once learned, will make things a great deal easier.

The first thing is that the pastry must be kept cool, or it all goes wrong. This is pretty easy if a food processor is used, rather than hot little hands. Use very cold ingredients, cool hands and, preferably, a cool kitchen.

The pastry needs to be kept flaky and short, rather than tough and elastic, or it shrinks in the oven and is generally unpalatable. The secret is to handle the pastry as little and as gently as possible after the liquid has been added to it.

Rolling the pastry out needs a little bit of technique. This really does improve with practice. Part of the secret is to allow the pastry to rest in the fridge before it is rolled. The other part is to flour the surface and rolling pin well, so that the pastry doesn't stick. Most tarts and pies are best made with a thin layer of pastry; however, it is best not to be too ambitious, at least to start with, and be satisfied with a medium thickness.

How to make pastry

The quantities I give below are enough for a shortcrust pastry tart of about 20–25cm/8–10in diameter, enough to feed six or eight. The basic principle is to use twice as much flour as fat, although I tend to use a little more butter. Once you've mastered the basic recipe, you can experiment with more or less of this or that, as I do. I tend to be generous on the ingredients, as it means I can roll out the pastry rather larger than the case and don't have to spend time mending cracks and holes at the edges. Any spare pastry can be used to make jam tarts.

• *A note on flour* ~ as I said in Chapter 2, I like to use 00 or superfine, as then I don't need to sift it; but if you use any other kind, do sift it first. This gets rid of any lumps and ensures there is enough air in it.

• *A note on water* ~ The amount of water needed will depend on the sort of flour you are using, and also the richness of the mixture. A rough guide is to use up to 1 tbsp per 25g/1oz of flour. However, this is not an exact figure. I often make large batches of pastry, using 425g/15oz of flour; and with different makes of flour and butter, even 100ml/3½fl oz water has sometimes been too wet. If you put in too much, the mixture will be unusable, or at any rate too damp to roll out (which is not a disaster; see 'Rolling the pastry' below). If you put in too little and have to add more after whizzing it up, you will need to whizz again, and the pastry will have been beaten more than is ideal. My advice is to use exactly the same ingredients and method each time, and after a little practice you will soon get the hang of precisely how much water you need.

Shortcrust Pastry

170g/6oz plain flour
85g/3oz butter, cold from the fridge

A few tbsp of cold water

Making the pastry
1. If you are a perfectionist, put the water in the freezer for 20 minutes to ensure that it is very cold.
2. Put the flour in the food processor with the cold butter, cut into about eight cubes. (If you don't have a food processor, see step 7.)
3. Process so that the flour and butter are thoroughly combined and look a little like breadcrumbs. It is important not to overdo the mixing. If you feel it is too warm, you can put the mixture in the fridge for 20 minutes to cool it down.
4. Add the water, sprinkling it over the pastry mixture. I do this when the food processor is on low, tipping the water in through the hole at the top. (See 'A note on water' above.)
5. Whizz up in the food processor again, but only briefly, a few tens of seconds only. Stop either when the mixture forms a ball, or preferably just before that, when the dough starts to pull away from the sides of the bowl.
6. Take the pastry out of the food processor and put it in the fridge, wrapped in clingfilm or a polythene bag, for 20 or 30 minutes at least. I think an hour is better, and it will come to no harm if you leave it for several hours. Resting the pastry not only keeps it cool, but also means that it is more elastic and pliable, so it rolls much better and does not crack so easily in the oven.
7. If you don't have a food processor, place the butter and flour in a large bowl and mix it either with a pastry blender – an implement with wires that helps to cut the butter into the flour – or with two knives, drawn across each other like rudimentary scissors. You can remove any remaining lumps of butter by rubbing them gently into the flour with your fingertips. Then gently stir the water in with a fork, one tablespoon at a time.

Rolling the pastry
1. To roll out the pastry you will need a clean, dry work surface. A marble slab is best, as it is cold and the pastry will not stick to it. Dust the surface, the rolling pin and the top of the pastry with a bit of plain flour, either by hand or through a sieve to give a light, even dusting. If your work surface is not as good as it should be, buy and use a plastic rolling surface (e.g. from Lakeland).

2. Roll out the pastry by rolling up and down and side to side, so that it spreads out into a circle. Press down less hard near the edges to avoid making the dough too thin. Perfection is not easy, and little cracks and holes often appear at the corners, which can be filled in as they develop. The pastry needs to be big enough to cover the bottom and sides of the tart case, so it has to be a bit bigger than the bottom of the tart case, normally by 2.5cm/1in or so. I tend to be generous in the overhang I allow, and just cut off the excess.

3. If the pastry is too damp, or the surface too rough or not floured sufficiently, it may stick to the surface. Try turning it in quarter turns as you roll. If the problem is acute, there is no easy cure. But if it is not too serious, a very large palette knife can be used to gently lift the pastry off the surface in one piece.

4. If it all goes wrong, you can start again; crunch the pastry up into a ball, possibly with a bit of water. This is not ideal, but it is slightly better than throwing it away.

Lining the tart case with the pastry

1. Place the pastry gently in the tart case, lining the base and sides. The best way to do this is to hang it over the rolling pin, although I do it by hand. Smooth it gently into the corners. Do not stretch to fit, or the pastry will shrink back during cooking.

2. Cut off the excess pastry around the top edge of the tart, cutting the pastry towards the outside of the tart rather than the inside. If there are gaps in the pastry, patch them with some of the excess; it sometimes doesn't stick very well, but this often improves during the cooking. You can help the patches to stick by moistening the edges to be stuck together with milk or egg white; little cooking brushes are good for this, or indeed any child's paintbrush (after it has been well cleaned, obviously).

And then...

1. It is very helpful to rest the pastry case in the fridge for half an hour or an hour. I often make the pastry case the day before and clap it overnight into the fridge or, preferably, the freezer.

2. Add the filling to the pastry case and cook. It is worth putting the tin on a baking tray that has already heated to oven temperature. This helps to ensure that the bottom of the tart cooks properly, using conduction rather than just convection, and it helps to avoid the common problem of having an uncooked bottom and burnt edges.

3. Generally, tarts are best eaten warm rather than hot, when they have been out of the oven for 10 or 20 minutes.

Some further tips and variations

• *Alternatives to rolling the pastry* ~ If you think that rolling out the pastry is beyond you, or the pastry is too damp to allow it, there are a number of alternative methods. They work better if the pastry is relatively moist. The pastry is a bit less even, but I don't think that matters too much.

1. Cut thinnish circles off a roll of pastry and lay them in the tart dish, butting circle up against circle.
2. With reasonably moist pastry, you can simply press the pastry into the tart tin by hand. I tend to do this when my pastry is wetter than I anticipated, and is therefore a bit difficult to roll without sticking unduly to the table.
3. Grate the pastry into the tart dish and pat down, making an even layer over the bottom and sides of the dish. This is particularly useful if your pastry is dry and won't roll out easily.

• *Increasing the quantities* ~ I often make two or three tart cases at the same time, or a pie and a tart, some to use that day or the next, and the rest to put in the freezer. It is very little more effort to make two or three rather than one. My standard ingredients for three 20–23cm/8–9in tarts are 425g/15oz flour, 250g/9oz butter (i.e. a pack) and 100–150ml/3–5fl oz water (though see 'A note on water' on p. 119). I tend to make medium-thin tarts, so these ingredients will be very generous if you are making only two tarts.

• *Spare pastry* ~ If you have any spare pastry, there is a good alternative to throwing it away. Make little tart cases to turn into jam tarts. They will be rather inelegant if patched together from bits and pieces, but this does not matter much. Add a large spoonful of jam to each tart. Children like doing this, particularly adding the jam, and they can then eat 'their' tart later. The jam tarts will take much less time to cook than a big one (about 20 minutes). Alternatively, you can make a savoury filling with, for instance, little bits of cheese, pancetta cubes and chopped tomatoes, separately or mixed.

• *Blind baking* ~ This means cooking the pastry without any filling in. It is necessary for fillings that either a) do not need cooking, or b) need less cooking than the pastry, or c) are quite liquid. The tart case is likely to rise like a balloon from air trapped under the pastry unless it is held down. To prevent this, you can prick the base with a fork before cooking; but the best way is to line the tart with greaseproof paper then fill the case with ceramic pastry beads or just with dried beans. An alternative – which I prefer – is simply to put some folded silver foil inside the tart case before cooking. I also fold the foil over the edge of the tart tin, which stops the edges cooking too quickly, and I often put some beads in the middle of the tart as well.

To blind bake, place the tart case in a preheated oven of 350F/180C/gas mark 4 and calculate your cooking times as follows:

- If the filling is not going to be cooked, remove the ceramic beans/silver foil after 30 minutes and cook the empty case for about another 15 minutes, by which time it should be lightly coloured. Alternatively just cook the tart for about 40 minutes in total, with the foil in, which is what I do.
- If the filling is going to be cooked, cook the empty pastry case for 15–30 minutes until lightly coloured, then allow it to cool a little before adding the filling. Put it back in the oven for as long as the recipe specifies.
- If your pastry is particularly thick, you may find that it will need a little more cooking time.

- *Cracked tarts* ~ Pastry tarts can sometimes crack a little, particularly if you blind bake them first. If you then add some very liquid contents, for instance custard, they will seep through. To avoid this, try coating the inside of the tart case with a brush dipped in some egg white before adding the contents.

Variations in ingredients

- *Rich shortcrust* ~ Increase the proportions of butter to flour from 1:2 up to about 2:3. Then add an egg (either a whole egg or just the yolk) after mixing the fat and flour, and before adding any water. A rich shortcrust, particularly with a whole egg, may in fact need little or even no water. This is a bit harder to roll out than normal shortcrust. I think rich shortcrust is particularly good for pastry that is going to be eaten cold.

- *Sweet pastry* ~ Sweet pastry, or pâté sucrée, is just ordinary or rich shortcrust pastry with some sugar added. Add up to a quarter of the weight of the flour in sugar, either icing or caster sugar. Mix the sugar in with the flour and butter before adding any egg or water.

• *Puff pastry* ~ This involves rolling enormous quantities of butter into the pastry. It is very tedious, time-consuming and fiddly and I have never bothered with it. It is much easier to buy the stuff, and frozen puff pastry can be good, at least if you buy some made with butter rather than vegetable oil.

• *What fat?* ~ The fat for pastry can be butter, hard margarine, lard or any combination of these. Personally, I do not like the distinctive taste of margarine, although it is a bit easier to use and is perfectly acceptable in shortcrust pastry. Lard on its own is not really suitable for pudding tarts, but it is easy to rub in and handle. Having experimented, I tend to make pâté sucrée with butter, and shortcrust pastry with either butter or half and half butter and lard. Some tarts are better with butter – a rich apple tart, for instance – and some, such as a mince tart, are perhaps better with half lard and half butter.

• *Alternatives to plain flour* ~ You can replace half the flour with wholemeal. A small amount of ground nuts can be used instead of the flour, again up to half. Almonds are particularly good, for instance if you are making a pear tart. The pastry is likely to be quite difficult to roll, so you might need to follow the alternative methods to rolling (see p. 122).

• *Alternative liquids* ~ Add a small amount of lemon or orange juice, say a quarter of a teaspoon, or indeed some grated lemon zest. Or try some vanilla extract, or a little yogurt or crème fraîche. Add these at the water stage (see step 4 of 'Making the pastry' above), and reduce or eliminate the water correspondingly.

Making pastry by hand

The traditional way to make pastry is by hand. Some people even now do not seem to realise that the invention of the food processor has revolutionised pastry-making. I have, though, ended up making a lot of tarts in a kitchen in the wilds of west Ireland without the benefit of modern appliances. If making pastry by hand (see p. 120, step 7), the fat will have to be near room temperature to be easy to work with. The great danger is that you might overheat the mixture. I find that using a pastry blender, an implement with wire loops, largely avoids this problem. When making by hand, it is essential to cool the pastry in the fridge for a time before rolling it out.

Cooking time
Generally speaking, tarts need about 375–425F/190–220C/gas mark 5–7
for about 45 minutes. Obviously, at the higher temperature the time will be
reduced, and at the lower increased. Some people suggest you start off at a
hotter temperature and move down to a lower one after 10 or 15 minutes; this
is not essential, but do experiment. In the recipes below I have given the mid-
temperature to avoid confusion, but it is worth trying it all ways.

It helps enormously to have a metal baking sheet already hot in the oven to
put the tart on; this avoids having thoroughly browned edges but an uncooked
base. You can tell when the tart is cooked by the fact that the edges look golden
or, better, slightly browned. If your tart is on the thick side, as mine often are,
you will need to cook it for longer. Beware of recipes with very short cooking
times: they may be fine for very thin pastry, but for the average clod-hopping
cook like me, they can produce inedible, uncooked pastry.

Apple Tart

This is enough for about six people.

**Like most fruit tarts, this is pretty straightforward. There are, of course, any
number of versions to choose from. My standard tart cuts as many corners
as possible, and is very easy.**

For the pastry:
170g/6oz plain flour
85g/3oz butter, cold from the fridge
For the filling:
60–115g/2–4oz butter
60g/2oz caster, soft brown or light
 muscovado sugar
1 tsp nutmeg or cinnamon (optional)

2 tsp cornflour, dissolved, or 60g/2oz
 plain flour
1 tsp vanilla extract
1 or 2 eggs, beaten
1 or 2 medium-sized cooking apples
 (or just use eating apples, which are
 a bit more tart)
1 Cox's apple (optional)

1. Make the pastry as explained on p. 120 and use to line the tart tin.
2. Put a baking tray in the oven, and heat to 400F/200C/gas mark 6.
3. To make the filling, put the butter in a large measuring jug or basin, and melt
 in the microwave in about four or five 10-second blasts.

4. Mix in the sugar, spices, cornflour (or flour), vanilla and eggs.
5. Peel all of the apples and grate them with a coarse grater, leaving only the core. Alternatively, core the apples and chop them into smallish slices.
6. Combine the apples and the other ingredients and put into the tart case.
7. Bake for about 45 minutes. The top should have browned a bit by the end.
8. Eat warm with cream.

Variation

• *A more proper French apple tart* ~ Use half a dozen or more largeish eating apples and up to 170g/6oz of apricot jam. Peel and core the apples and cut them up, cutting half of them into elegant slices. Cook half the apples (i.e. not the elegant slices) gently with half of the apricot jam and a few tablespoons of water until tender, and then purée in a food processor. Spread the mixture on the base of the tart. Arrange on top the remaining slices of apple. Gently heat the rest of the apricot jam with 1 tbsp water in a pan and boil for a minute or two until thickened. Use this to glaze the apples, and then cook the tart for 45 minutes. The apples that are cooked first and puréed can be cooking apples. Alternatively, you can use a frangipane mixture (see Bakewell tart, below), perhaps with some Calvados added, to make a tarte Normande.

Bakewell Tart and other frangipane tarts

Sufficient for six people.

Traditionally known as Bakewell pudding, Bakewell tart originally did not contain ground almonds. The mixture of equal quantities of butter, sugar and ground almonds (with optional eggs) is known as frangipane, and is used in other tarts and puddings, too. It is very easy to make.

For the pastry:
170g/6oz plain flour
85g/3oz butter, cold from the fridge
For the filling:
115g/4oz good raspberry jam
115g/4oz butter
115g/4oz sugar

115g/4oz ground almonds
3 eggs
15–25g/½–1 oz flour, either plain or self-raising (optional)
½ tsp almond extract (optional)
60g/2oz flaked almonds (optional)

1. Make the pastry as explained on p. 120 and use it to line the tart tin.
2. Put a baking tray in the oven and heat the oven to 400F/200C/gas mark 6.
3. Spread the raspberry jam over the tart base.
4. Mix the remaining ingredients except for the flaked almonds in a food processor until smooth. If you are being fancy, cream the butter and sugar first and then add the remaining ingredients.
5. Put this frangipane mixture in the tart base on top of the jam.
6. Bake in the oven for about 45 minutes. The tart should be golden and feel set.
7. If you like, add some flaked almonds on top, about 10 minutes before the pudding is cooked so they brown a little.
8. Eat hot or cold, on its own or with cream, vanilla ice cream or custard.

Variations

• *Alcohol* ~ Add a suitable liqueur, a tablespoon or so, and perhaps a tablespoon or two of cream.

• *Almond tart* ~ Use just the frangipane mixture without any jam. You will need to double the quantities.

• *Blackberry and pear* ~ Don't add any jam. Add to the frangipane mixture a couple of pears, peeled, cored and cut into quarters or eighths, and a handful or two of blackberries. Plain pear tart without blackberries is also very good.

• *Cherries* ~ Instead of the jam, use cherries. You will need about 450g/1lb cherries, which need to be stoned. Press the cherries into the top of the frangipane mixture before cooking. A tablespoon of kirsch is a good addition; stir it into the mixture.

• *Fruit* ~ Almost any fruit can be added to the frangipane mixture (without the jam underneath), for instance apricots (which go especially well with almonds, of course), greengages, nectarines, peaches, plums or strawberries. As long as they are ripe, they don't need cooking first.

• *Jam* ~ Try apricot jam instead.

• *Lemon curd* ~ Use lemon curd instead of the jam. If adventurous, you can make your own lemon curd, too.

• *Raspberries* ~ Scatter about 350g/12oz raspberries over the already jammed tart base before covering with the frangipane mixture. Reduce or eliminate the jam if desired.

• *Rhubarb* ~ Add about 2–4 sticks of rhubarb, chopped into small pieces, to the pudding, pressing them in a tasteful pattern after the filling has been added to the tart. This is even better if you add the finely grated zest of a lemon to the frangipane mixture.

Chocolate Tart

This should be enough for six to eight people.

There are almost infinite variations of this pudding, which is hardly surprising given how popular chocolate is with almost everyone. My chocolate tart is very simple to make; many are extremely complicated.

For the pastry:
170g/6oz plain flour
85g/3oz butter, cold from the fridge
For the filling:
85–115g/3–4oz sugar

5 whole eggs (you can use 2 egg yolks
  and 3 whole eggs)
1 tsp vanilla extract (entirely optional)
225g/8oz good dark chocolate
140g/5oz butter

1. Make the pastry as explained on p. 120 and use it to line the tart tin. This should be quite a high-sided tart, as the filling comes up a good 1cm/½ in.
2. Put a baking tray in the oven, and heat to 400F/200C/gas mark 6.
3. Fill the tart with baking beans or foil (see p. 122–3). Bake for about 25–30 minutes on the baking tray. You can remove the beans after 15 minutes or leave them in, as you prefer.
4. Meanwhile, about 10 minutes before the tart case is ready, beat the sugar and eggs together, preferably using an electric whisk. The ingredients should be well beaten together. Add the vanilla, if using.
5. Break up the chocolate, cut the butter up, and melt both. Add the melted chocolate and butter to the egg and sugar mixture, and mix well.
6. Remove the tart from the oven and allow it to cool a little.
7. Add the chocolate mixture carefully to the tart case and cook for a further

20–25 minutes at a slightly lower temperature, e.g. 350F/180C/gas mark 5. Keep the tray in the oven to catch any overspill. The tart is done when it is set, but not too set. It is often difficult to have the centre cooked enough and the chocolate near the edges not overdone.

8. Serve warm or at room temperature, with cream or ice cream (vanilla or chocolate).

Tips

• *Melting the chocolate and butter* ~ The traditional method is to put them in a small pan and heat over a low flame, stirring until melted. It is easier to melt them in the microwave, perhaps four bursts of 20 or 30 seconds at a time. The chocolate takes longer to melt, so start heating this first and add the butter when the chocolate is starting to look gooey at the edges.

• *A simple alternative* ~ A lazy way is to start with the melted chocolate and butter, add the sugar and vanilla and mix in, then add the five eggs and mix them in, too.

Variations

• *Cocoa* ~ This can be added to the pastry to enhance the taste of chocolate. Or add about 60g/2oz to the chocolate mixture to make it a bit more solid.

• *Cream* ~ Add to the butter or replace it with up to 300ml/10fl oz double cream.

• *Eggs* ~ Some recipes reduce the eggs to two or three, but there is a danger of the mixture not setting properly.

• *Milk chocolate* ~ You can replace some or all of the dark chocolate with milk chocolate. Using only dark chocolate can be a bit too grown-up for children.

• *Other* ~ All the obvious things can be added, for instance a small amount of an appropriate liqueur, or a small slug of rum, or some strong coffee, or some grated orange zest.

• *Quantities* ~ I have tried one and a half times this quantity of filling in two tarts (i.e. double the pastry quantity given here), but making the tarts less high at the sides, which works quite well.

Custard Tart

Enough for six people.

For the pastry:
170g/6oz plain flour
85g/3oz butter, cold from the fridge
For the filling:
300ml/10fl oz single or double cream
1–2 tsp mace, cinnamon or nutmeg

4 eggs, 2 of them separated
25g/1oz sugar (or 1–2 tsp honey)
1 tsp vanilla extract
2 tsp orange flower water or rose
　water (optional but very desirable)

1. Make the tart case (see p. 120) and blind bake it (see p. 122–3) in a preheated oven at 400F/200C/gas mark 6 for 15 minutes. Take it out and lower the temperature to 325F/160C/gas mark 3.
2. Bring the cream and spices to the boil in a pan (or keep the nutmeg to dust the top later).
3. In a bowl, combine two eggs and two egg yolks with the sugar, vanilla and orange flower water. Pour in the cream and spice mixture and stir to mix.
4. Brush the tart case with one of the leftover egg whites.
5. Pour the custard mixture into the tart case. It is easiest to do this while the tart is in the oven, to avoid spillage. Do not fill right to the brim or it will spill.
6. Cook in the oven for about 30–40 minutes. The custard should be set, but not too set, and you must be careful not to overcook it.

Fruit Tart

Enough for six people.

This is a good tart for warm summer days. I suppose it is not really a proper pudding, but rather a dessert.

For the pastry:
170g/6oz plain flour
85g/3oz butter, cold from the fridge
For the filling:
60g/2oz sugar (optional)

450g/1lb mascarpone, or a mixture
　of mascarpone and double cream
450g/1lb fruit, such as strawberries
Sugar to taste, about 25–60g/1–2oz

1. Make the pastry as explained on p. 120 and use it to line the tart tin.
2. Blind bake (see p. 122–3) in a preheated oven at 400F/200C/gas mark 6 for about 40 minutes until entirely cooked.
3. Allow the tart to cool, which will take an hour or so. It is easy enough to make the tart the day before and keep it overnight in a sealed plastic box or tin.
4. If you are using double cream with the mascarpone, then beat them together.
5. Beat the sugar into the mascarpone.
6. Spread the mascarpone evenly over the tart base. If you want to, sprinkle some more sugar over this, to taste.
7. Add the fruit. You can cut it up and arrange delicately, if fussy.
8. Sprinkle some sugar over the top, if you like.
9. Eat cold, on its own.

Some other ideas

These are all pretty similar in terms of what you do, though some fruit needs a bit of cooking before adding to the tart. I will be pretty brief in describing what to do, assuming that you have tried some of the other fruit tarts described later in this chapter. Redcurrant jelly is a good glaze for many fruit tarts.

• *Apricot tart* ~ Take 900g/2lb apricots, cut in half and remove the stones. Mix with 25–60g/1–2oz sugar and 1 tsp or so of vanilla extract. Add to the tart case and cook as above. Apricots are good in a frangipane mixture (see under Bakewell tart, p. 126).

• *Blackcurrant tart* ~ Take 675g/1½lb blackcurrants and 170g/6oz sugar. Cook together gently for a few minutes, then boil quite hard until it becomes a reasonably gloopy mess, which will take only a few minutes more. Cool down before adding to the tart, and then cook in the oven as above. This is much better with a pastry lattice on top, which is unfortunate, as they are fiddly to do, but one does need a bit more pastry to balance the intense taste. Cut strips of pastry and lay them across the top in a lattice pattern, sealing at the edges. An easier alternative is simply to make blackcurrant pie. This tart is good with pâte sucrée, i.e. sweet pastry (see p. 123). Try adding, say, 3 tsp cinnamon.

• *Cherry tart* ~ Try 675g/1½lb cherries, 60g/2oz sugar, and perhaps a couple of teaspoons of Calvados. The cherries will need to be stoned first. Cherries are good in an egg custard mixture; reduce the quantity of cherries a little and add

300ml/10fl oz of double cream and three eggs to the mixture. Cherries are also good in a frangipane mixture (see under Bakewell tart, p. 126).

• *Pear tart* ~ Peel, core and chop 900g/2lb pears and mix with some sugar, about 60g/2oz. Some suggest that the pears should be stewed first for a few minutes and then drained, but I don't think this is necessary. As for possible additions, try a couple of spoonfuls of double cream, some chopped walnuts and some vanilla extract or cinnamon. Or add some ginger, or lemon zest and juice.

Lemon Tart

Enough for about six to eight people.

This is a pretty easy tart to make, straightforward to prepare and relatively difficult to screw up entirely. The big issue is how lemony to make the tart: some people make it so you can barely detect the lemon, others so that the lemon takes off the roof of your mouth. I try for something in the middle.

For the pastry:
170g/6oz plain flour
85g/3oz butter, cold from the fridge
For the filling:
3 lemons

5 egg yolks
170g/6oz caster sugar, or to taste (this quantity is not particularly sweet)
1 tsp vanilla extract (optional)
150ml/5fl oz double cream (optional)

1. Make the pastry as explained on p. 120 and use it to line a tart tin.
2. Blind bake the pastry (see p. 122–3) in a preheated oven at 400F/200C/ gas mark 6 for about 20 minutes. Remove from the oven and lower the temperature to 300F/150C/gas mark 2.
3. Meanwhile, grate the zest of one of the lemons and juice all three.
4. Beat the egg yolks lightly together with a fork.
5. Add the grated lemon zest, lemon juice and egg yolks to the remaining ingredients and mix.
6. Pour the mixture into the pastry case and cook for about 20 minutes until just set. The tart will continue to set once it is removed from the oven.
7. Eat hot, warm or cold. Warm is probably best, as with most tarts.

Variations

• *General* ~ You can vary the ingredients quite a lot. The vanilla and cream are optional, but I think they are a good idea. You could add some melted butter as well as (or instead of) the cream, up to 140g/5oz. You can vary the number of egg yolks, preferably upwards rather than downwards (or the tart will not set properly), and you can replace some of the egg yolks with whole eggs.

• *Almonds* ~ Add 85g/3oz ground almonds to make a lemon and almond tart. The almonds do make the tart taste very much less lemony. However, instead of a brilliant yellow colour, it will be a rather dull brown, which is a disadvantage for those who care about looks.

• *Brulée* ~ It can be quite fun to allow the lemon tart to cool, sprinkle 1–2 tbsp caster sugar on the top and melt the sugar with a blowtorch.

• *Lime* ~ Try replacing one of the lemons with a lime for a slightly different taste. The tart tends to look even more lemony.

Lemon Meringue Pie

Sufficient for six people.

OK, I know it's called a pie, but this is really a tart. LMP is more complicated to make than most, but it's well worth it. There is nothing quite like the balance between the tart, the lemony filling and the meringue, which should be crisp outside and soft inside. Regarding lemon quantities, I think three is too lemony and the best balance is the juice of two lemons and the zest of three.

For the pastry:
170g/6oz plain flour
85g/3oz butter, cold from the fridge
For the filling:
3 level tbsp cornflour (I know it
  sounds a lot)
300–425ml/10–15fl oz water or milk
Grated zest and juice of 2–3 lemons

3–4 eggs
60g/2oz butter, cut into smallish
  cubes or melted
80–115g/3–4oz caster sugar to taste
(I like it sweet)
For the meringue:
115–170g/4–6oz caster sugar

1. Make the pastry as explained on p. 120 and use it to line a tart tin, preferably one with quite high edges.
2. Blind bake the pastry (see p. 122–3) for about 20 minutes in a preheated oven at 400F/200C/gas mark 6. Take out and lower the temperature to 300F/150C/gas mark 2. If there are holes or cracks in the case, brush with an egg white to stop the mixture escaping after you put it in.
3. Separate the eggs; set the whites aside for the meringue. Lightly whisk the egg yolks.
4. Dissolve the cornflour in some of the water or milk to make a paste.
5. Add the grated lemon zest and juice, and the rest of the water or milk.
6. Bring the mixture to the boil and cook for a couple of minutes. Allow to cool for a few minutes.
7. Add the whisked egg yolks, the melted (or chopped-up) butter and the sugar and mix together. Pour this into the pastry shell.
8. For the meringue, whisk the egg whites until they form stiff peaks. This is quite hard work unless you use an electric mixer.
9. Whisk the caster sugar into the meringue, a quarter or half of the quantity at a time.
10. Use a broad-bladed knife to spread the meringue across the top of the pudding to the edge of the pastry rim, so that it seals the top.
11. Cook in the oven for 30–40 minutes, until the top is golden but not burnt.
12. Serve. It needs no accompaniment, not even custard, I regret to say.

Variations
The basic idea of a meringue pie with something fruity in the middle can be used for a variety of insides.

• *Apple and lemon meringue pie* ~ For the filling, use 450g/1lb cooking apples, peeled, cored and sliced, the zest and juice of one lemon, three egg yolks and 85g/3oz sugar. Cook the apples and lemon zest and juice in a pan over a low heat for about 10 minutes. Lightly whisk the egg yolks and add them and the sugar to the apples. Pour the mixture into the pastry case and cover with meringue, cooking as above. As the contents are quite lemony, this is just an easy variation on lemon meringue pie.

• *Apricot meringue pie* ~ For the filling, use 450g/1lb stoned apricots, the zest and juice of a lemon, two or three egg yolks, 25g/1oz melted butter and 50g/2oz sugar. Cook the apricots in a little water on a low heat for about 10 minutes. You may want to push the apricots through a sieve at this stage. Add the remaining ingredients and proceed as above.

• *Orange meringue pie* ~ Substitute the zest and juice of one or two oranges for the lemons, and perhaps a little lemon juice, too. I think two oranges are better for taste. The water will need to be reduced accordingly, depending on the size of the oranges, probably by about half.

Rhubarb Meringue Pie

Serves about six people.

I have adapted this from a very good Nigella Lawson recipe. This recipe is somewhat more straightforward than for a lemon meringue pie. It is particularly delicious with early-season rhubarb. It is sufficiently different in method to need full instructions.

For the pastry:
170g/6oz plain flour
85g/3oz butter, cold from the fridge
For the filling:
675g/1½lbs rhubarb
Juice of a small orange (orange juice from a carton will do)

4 eggs, separated (keep the whites for the meringue)
140g/5oz caster sugar
60g/2oz of plain flour
60g/2oz butter, melted
For the meringue:
115–170g/4–6oz caster sugar

1. Make the pastry as explained on p. 120, and use it to line a tart tin, preferably one with quite high edges.
2. Blind bake the pastry (see p. 122–3) in a preheated oven at 400F/200C/gas mark 6 for about 20 minutes.
3. Chop the rhubarb into pieces about 1cm/½in or less.
4. Put the rhubarb and orange juice into a pan and heat on a moderately gentle heat for about five to 10 minutes, stirring occasionally. The rhubarb should not be reduced to pulp, only made slightly softer.
5. Meanwhile mix together the egg yolks, sugar, flour and butter. It is easiest to melt the butter in a microwave, 10 or 20 seconds at a time.

6. Pour off the juice from the rhubarb. Add as much of this juice as is needed to the eggy mixture to make a soft paste.

7. Transfer the rhubarb to the pastry case, cover with the sugary mixture, and cook for a further 20 minutes until it starts to set.

8. Remove the tart from the oven and lower the temperature to 300F/150C/gas mark 2.

9. While the tart is cooking, make the meringue. Whisk the egg whites until they form stiff peaks. This is quite hard work unless you use an electric whisk.

10. Whisk the caster sugar into the meringue, a quarter or half at a time.

11. Use a broad-bladed knife to spread the meringue across the top of the pudding to the edge of the pastry rim, so it seals the top.

12. Cook in the oven for about 20 minutes, until the meringue is golden but not burnt.

Plum Tart

Enough for six people.

The danger with plum tarts is that if the case is properly cooked, the plums may be overcooked. One solution is to blind bake the case for 10 minutes first. The obvious complement to plums are almonds, and thus they go well with frangipane (a mixture of ground almonds, sugar and butter; see Bakewell tart, p. 126). They also go well with apricots, thus a mixture of plums and apricots is good, or one can use apricot jam as a glaze on a plum tart, though this is a bit posh for me. I sometimes make a very simple but elegant plum tart, which goes down well with people of refined taste who wouldn't contemplate a plum duff: mothers-in-law and suchlike. Here it is.

For the pastry:
170g/6oz plain flour
85g/3oz butter, cold from the fridge
1 egg

For the filling:
450–700g/1–1½lb plums
25g/1oz caster sugar

1. Make the pastry as explained on p. 120, including an egg in the mixture. Line a tart tin with the pastry and blind bake (see p. 122–3) in a preheated oven at 400F/200C/gas mark 6 for about 10 minutes. Remove from the oven.

2. Meanwhile, slice or halve the plums, removing the stones. I tend to cut off the very ends of the fruit, which are more skin than plum. Place them in the cooked tart case and cook for a further 20 minutes.
3. Take the tart out of the oven and sprinkle the plums with the caster sugar. Return to the oven for a further 10 minutes.
4. Serve warm with cream.

Variation
• *Plum and almond* ~ Here is a less elegant version with almonds. The ingredients, in addition to the shortcrust pastry case, are: 675g/1½lb plums, stoned and roughly cut up; 1 tbsp cornflour; 1 tsp cinnamon; 85g/3oz sugar, white or brown; and 85g/3oz almonds, either ground or small flakes. Dissolve the cornflour in a little water. Mix all the filling ingredients together in a bowl. Put in the tart case and cook as above for about 40 minutes; or blind bake the case for 10 minutes first, add the filling and cook for another 30 minutes.

Rhubarb Tart

For a normal tart for about six.

For the pastry:
170g/6oz plain flour
85g/3oz butter, cold from the fridge

For the filling:
450g/1lb rhubarb
115g/4oz of sugar

1. Make the pastry as explained on p. 120 and use it to line a tart tin.
2. Put a baking tray in the oven and preheat the oven to 400F/200C/gas mark 6.
3. Cut the rhubarb up into pieces 1cm/½in long or smaller and put in the tart tin with the sugar.
4. Cook for about 40 minutes. Sprinkling a tablespoon of brown sugar over the tart halfway through is quite nice.
5. Serve. This tart is particularly good with custard, I think, but cream or crème fraîche will do.

One potential problem is that rhubarb produces quite a lot of liquid, which can drip out a bit when the tart is cut. I do not think this really matters, but to avoid it you can gently cook the rhubarb on the hob first for about five minutes with the sugar until soft, and then drain most of the rhubarb juice off, using it later as a sauce for the tart, if you like. If you follow this method, you can also try blind baking the tart for 10 minutes before cooking it for another 20–30 minutes with the fruit inside. The problem can also be reduced or avoided by adding ground almonds or frangipane (see variations below).

Variations
You can use any of the variations for rhubarb crumble (see p. 49); for instance, add a couple of teaspoons of ginger. I also recommend the following.

• *Rhubarb and almond* ~ Add about 85–115g/3–4oz of ground almonds to the rhubarb and sugar, mixing well, before putting the mixture in the tart. The sugar should be reduced a little, say to 60–85g/2–3oz. A couple of teaspoons of ginger can also be added.

• *Rhubarb and frangipane* ~ See Bakewell tart (p. 126).

• *Rhubarb and strawberry* ~ This is a particularly delicious tart. Use half and half of each fruit.

Tarte Tatin

Will feed about six people.

This is basically an upside down apple tart, usually with the sugar cooked for a few minutes on the top of the stove at the start in order to caramelise it. This makes a most delicious tart, which almost everyone likes. Tarte Tatin is basically pretty easy, and you are mad not to try it if you have mastered how to make a tart. It was, apparently, first invented by mistake by the Tatin sisters in Lamotte-Beuveron in the Loire region more than a century ago.

Most tart tins are not ideal for caramelising the sugar on the top of the stove. You need either a thick tarte Tatin tin, or a sauté pan. I have used an ordinary tart tin a few times without any problems. However, a loose-bottomed tart tin is definitely not suitable for caramelising the sugar, or for cooking in the oven either, as it allows the sugary mixture to leak out.

For the pastry:
170g/6oz plain flour
85g/3oz butter, cold from the fridge
For the filling:
450–900g/1–2lb dessert apples

60–115g/2–4oz butter
60–115g/2–4oz caster sugar
Juice of ½ lemon (optional)
1 tsp cinnamon or other spice
(optional)

1. Make the pastry as on p. 120, and roll it out into a circle about 1cm/½in or so larger than your tart tin. Put clingfilm in the base of the tin; this is to make it easier to take the tart out of the tin at step 2. Arrange the pastry in the tart tin so that it comes up the sides by about 1cm/½in or so. Put some clingfilm on the top of the tart, too, to stop it drying out too much. Put it back in the fridge for at least half an hour; it can happily be left for hours.
2. Take the tart tin out of the fridge, remove the pastry case gently from it and put the pastry back in the fridge.
3. Sprinkle the sugar evenly in the base of the tart tin, and place on the hob over a medium or high heat until it has caramelised, which will be a few minutes.
4. When sufficiently caramelised, remove from the heat. Leave for 10 minutes.
5. Add the butter, cut into thinnish strips, to the tin. The butter will melt.
6. Preheat the oven to 400F/200C/gas mark 6.
7. Peel, core and slice the apples into moderately large slices (i.e. for eating apples, probably into eighths or less). If using lemon juice, squeeze it over the apples and mix. If you are using spices, sprinkle them over the fruit and mix.
8. By this time, the tart tin should have cooled down a bit. Arrange the apples in the tart tin. The apples should be pretty tightly packed.
9. After removing all the clingfilm (this is ESSENTIAL), place the pastry case upside down on top of the apples, and tuck the edges down the sides of the tin, so that when later inverted the pastry will hold the apple mixture.
10. Make a couple of holes with a knife in the pastry so that steam can escape while cooking.
11. Cook in the oven for about 45 minutes until light brown. Unlike most tarts, you can tell very easily if this one is cooked or not.
12. Leave to cool for five minutes, then invert onto a plate. If you do this too soon it will be too hot; if you wait too long the tart will have started to stick to the bottom and will not come out in one piece. Personally, I do not see anything wrong in serving the tart upside down, but everyone else does.
13. Serve with crème fraîche (which I think is preferable), cream, ice cream or custard.

Alternative methods
- For a relatively uncaramelised tarte Tatin, do not cook the sugar at all on the top of the stove. Instead, arrange the apples, sugar and butter on the bottom of the tin, cover with pastry and cook in the oven.
- Caramelise the sugar, butter and apples all together before putting on the pastry case. The mixture will need to be stirred a bit with a wooden spoon.
- Put the apple mixture already covered with pastry on the hob for a few minutes. I think this is a bit risky, as it is hard to tell how the apple mixture is getting on underneath the tart.
- The normal instruction is to place the rolled pastry on the apple, sugar and butter mixture, folding the edges round to make an upside down tart. I think this leads to crinkly thick edges, hence my preference for using a formed tart.

Some tips
- *Caramelising* ~ You may find that parts of the sugar base caramelise before other parts, and they may go too brown. I use a wooden spoon to mix up the caramelising mixture as I go along to ensure a relatively even consistency, or I take the tin off the hob with some oven gloves and gently wiggle it about so the molten sugar spreads over the whole base. Caramelised sugar will stick to any spoon, and when cool it can be given to a small child to suck.

- *How caramelised?* ~ While the amount of caramelisation is a matter of taste, I go for a golden colour. If you use a thick tarte Tatin tin, the caramelisation will continue for a little after it is taken off the heat, so remove the tin as soon as the sugar starts to go golden. If you overcook and burn the sugar, then getting the bits off is something of a pain. A little bit of burning may not actually ruin the tart. This whole process is not difficult, but a little bit of practice may be necessary to get it right.

- *Arranging the apples* ~ The apple pieces can be delicately arranged in the tart tin, but you might think this is *de trop*. Furthermore, the mixture often sticks to the tin a bit when cooked, and needs to be scraped out and blobbed about the tart, so any delicate arrangement will often be ruined.

Variations on ingredients
- *Apples* ~ Use crisp eating apples such as Cox's. Granny Smiths are probably the very best. Cooking apples are OK.

- *General* ~ As with most recipes, the relative proportions are somewhat flexible: I have seen some that double the amount of butter and sugar.

- *Sugar* ~ Light or dark brown sugar can be used. I tend to be generous in the quantity of sugar and use caster, which caramelises much more easily.

Other Tatins

The same method can be used for other fruit. Here are some examples.

- *Apricot* ~ Replace the apples with apricots, halved or quartered. They can be either fresh or tinned (and drained). Here are three suggestions for making it a bit more interesting. First, add a spoonful of Benedictine or Cointreau to the fruit mixture. Secondly, add 25–60g/1–2oz ground almonds and 1–2 tsp vanilla extract to the fruit mixture. Thirdly, after turning the finished tart upside down, add about 25g/1oz pine nuts, which have been carefully toasted in a dry frying pan.

- *Blackberry and apple* ~ Try 225g/8oz blackberries and 450g/1lb apples. This looks and tastes wonderful, and is perhaps the best Tatin of all.

- *Cherry* ~ Try 450–675g/1–1½lb cherries, stoned.

- *Peach* ~ Replace the apples with ripe peaches, halved or quartered. Vanilla extract is a nice addition.

- *Pear* ~ Replace the apples with 450–900g/1–2lb of pears, peeled and cored and cut into quarters or halves, arranged prettily in a cartwheel if you like. The pears don't need to be ripe, and they are easier to peel and cut up if they are not. It is a good idea to add the juice of half a lemon to the pears, or else the tart is lacking an essential bite. If you do not want to add lemon juice, try serving the pear Tatin with crème fraîche, which should supply the necessary tang. In addition, I think that pear tarte Tatin can be improved in the following two ways.

- *Pear and almonds* ~ Scatter 25–60g/1–2oz toasted flaked almonds on the cooked pear tarte Tatin. Alternatively, add twice this amount of ground almonds at the start. The ground almonds need to be mixed up in the butter that has melted above the caramelised sugar, but only when it has cooled a bit. If the ground almonds are added above the pear and thus next to the tart, this will make the tart much thicker and wudgier. Yet another alternative, which I think is the best, is to make the tart with some ground almonds, using them in place of some of the flour, say a third or a half of it.

• *Pear and ginger* ~ Add 1 tsp ground ginger early on. Or try two or three ginger balls in syrup, cutting the balls up into small pieces first. Add about 2–3 tbsp of the syrup along with the butter to the caramelised sugar, and stir in. Then arrange the pears, and scatter over the ginger pieces. Add the tart casing and cook in the oven. Alternatively, just add lots of chopped fresh ginger.

• *Rhubarb* ~ In addition to replacing the apples with rhubarb, chopped into pieces, I recommend the following changes to the normal apple recipe, although only the first is really necessary. First, it is a good idea to increase the sugar from 60g/2oz to 85–115g/3–4oz, and the additional sugar can be brown and should be added to the rhubarb. Secondly, the butter can be reduced or eliminated, although I tend to keep it. Thirdly, a teaspoon or two of ground ginger can be added to the rhubarb, and stirred in. Fourthly, I prefer to cook the rhubarb in a saucepan for five or 10 minutes to soften it, before adding in the extra sugar and the ginger, and then putting it in the tart tin on top of the caramelised sugar and butter.

Treacle Tart

Enough for six people.

This is a very traditional English tart, which goes down well almost universally, particularly with children. It should be thin, I think, but with lots of filling.

For the pastry:
170g/6oz plain flour
85g/3oz butter, cold from the fridge
For the filling:
450g/1lb golden syrup

115–170g/4–6oz fresh breadcrumbs
½ tsp lemon juice (optional)
3 tbsp double cream (optional)
1 tbsp black treacle

1. Make the pastry as explained on p. 120, and use it to line a 23-25cm/9-10in tart tin.
2. In a bowl, combine all the ingredients for the filling.
3. Leave the mixture to stand for at least quarter of an hour so that the breadcrumbs can absorb the syrup.
4. Preheat the oven to 400F/200C/gas mark 6, with a baking sheet to catch any overflowing treacle.
5. Transfer the treacle mixture to the tart case.
6. Bake in the oven for about 45 minutes. Treacle tart should be well cooked, so that the filling is sticky.
7. Eat, preferably with cold vanilla ice cream, which sets off the treacle tart beautifully. Alternatively, eat with cream, custard or crème fraîche.

Tips
Syrup is sticky and thus difficult to transfer from the tin to the basin. The most straightforward way to do this is to put a bowl on the scales and spoon in the syrup. Best of all, if you are using a 450g/1lb tin of the stuff, just hold it upside down for a while. It is very sticky and does not come out easily. Most authorities seem to think that it is easiest to use heated-up syrup, and it is certainly much easier to spoon in like this. Unfortunately, you cannot use the microwave to do this, for obvious reasons, so you need to warm it in some water on the hob; watch out for burning. I think it is too much trouble.

My favourite way of getting syrup out of the tin is to have two half-full tins, and balance them upside down against each other inside the bowl and let them drip for 10 minutes. It reminds me of my father's way of getting out the inside of large clams in the Far East, many years ago when it was acceptable to remove them from the sea. He used to tie them upside down in a tree with string, and a gooey mass would gradually fall out over a couple of weeks, much to the delight of the local ants.

Additions and variations
Many recipes use much less syrup and breadcrumb mixture than I tend to do, some use much more. It is worth experimenting to find out what you like best. While strictly optional, I almost always include the lemon, double cream and black treacle, for the reasons given below.

• *Black treacle* ~ A spoonful of this gives the tart a nice flavour.

• *Breadcrumbs* ~ Try brown breadcrumbs instead of white. A mixture works as well. If you are being particularly earthmotherish, you can use wholemeal flour to make the pastry, but I think that is going too far.

• *Butter* ~ Try 60g/2oz melted butter in the mixture.

• *Double cream* ~ The addition of a dollop of cream greatly helps to make the tart moist.

• *Egg* ~ Add an egg to the mixture.

• *Ginger* ~ Try ½–1 tsp ground ginger. I like adding a large quantity of chopped root ginger. This is delicious, but the pudding should be described as ginger and treacle tart to avoid a breach of the Trades Descriptions Act.

• *Lemon* ~ Some lemon is a good idea, as it cuts through the sweetness of the syrup. I think that under half a lemon's worth is quite enough, but try the grated zest and juice of up to one lemon. Some of the juice can be used instead of some of the water to make a lemony pastry. Too much juice and zest is a bit overpowering, and it does not go down well with some, particularly children.

• *Peel* ~ Add 60g/2oz chopped mixed peel instead of the lemon.

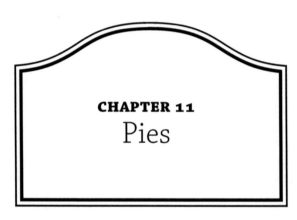

CHAPTER 11
Pies

IF YOU have mastered making a tart, then pies should hold little terror. I am going to go easy on the pie recipes, but generally any tart filling can be used for a pie and vice versa, except, of course, those that require blind baking, which you can't do with pies. Custard seems to go better with pies than with tarts.

How to make a pie
Making a pie is just like making a tart, with a few knobs on, so follow the recipe and all the tips for shortcrust pastry on p. 120, but increase the quantities as follows:

285g/10oz plain flour, preferably 00   A few tbsp cold water
140g/5oz butter, cold from the fridge

1. Make the pastry as explained on p. 120. Divide the just-made pastry into two pats, one slightly larger than the other, and put them in the fridge to rest for 20–30 minutes. The larger piece will form the bottom of the pie, and the smaller one the top.
2. Roll out the larger pat until it is at least 2.5cm/1in larger than the pie dish. Ease it into the dish, making sure there is pastry hanging over the pie dish lip. Then add the filling.
3. Roll out the other piece of pastry. To seal the top to the bottom, use a brush and some milk or water to moisten the pastry that is resting on the pie lip.
4. Lay the pastry lid over the dish and press the edges together with a fork.
5. Trim off any overhanging pastry with a sharp knife.
6. Cut a hole or two in the top of the pie to let some steam out.
7. Place a baking sheet in the oven to heat up and place the pie on it. This is particularly important, as it ensures that the bottom cooks as much as the top. Cook according to the recipe instructions. The oven temperature should be between 375–425F/190–220C/gas mark 5–7, but I have given the mid-temperature throughout for simplicity.

Incidentally, when a recipe says 225g/8oz of pastry, it normally means pastry made with 225g/8oz of flour, so the recipes below are for roughly 285g/10oz of pastry, for which I would use no more than 100ml/3½fl oz water. If you think you will need a bit more or a bit less pastry, increase or reduce the quantity in proportion – e.g. 225g/8oz flour and 115g/4oz butter. It doesn't have to be exactly twice as much flour as fat; I often use 25g/1oz or so more of butter.

Apple Pie

Serves about eight people.

Some of the cooking apples can be replaced with eating apples if you like, but it probably goes without saying that Bramleys are best.

For the pastry:
285g/10oz plain flour
140g/5oz butter, cold from the fridge
A few tbsp cold water
For the filling:
900g/2lb cooking apples

115–140g/4–5oz sugar
To glaze (optional):
Milk or an egg white
25g/1oz caster sugar

1. Make the pastry (see p. 120). Roll it out into two pieces as explained on p. 146 and use the larger piece to line the base and sides of a pie dish.
2. Heat the oven to 400F/200C/gas mark 6 and place a baking sheet in the oven.
3. Peel, core and slice the apples.
4. Add the apples to the pie dish and sprinkle the sugar over them.
5. Fix on the pie top and make a couple of holes in the middle of it with a knife.
6. Brush the pastry lid with milk or egg white and sprinkle on some caster sugar.
7. Cook for about 45 minutes until the top is crisp and golden.
8. Allow to cool a little and serve with cream, ice cream or custard.

Some variations
Plain apple pie can be a little dull and the following variations are distinct improvements.

• *Blackberry and apple* ~ I think this is my favourite pie, indeed it is one of the few serious rivals to steamed ginger and syrup sponge pudding with custard. One can eat it for only a few short weeks in September when the blackberries are ripe, unless one freezes the blackberries, which fortunately works quite well. All you need to do is replace about a third of the apples with blackberries.

• *Cheese* ~ While it sounds odd to have cheese in a pudding, apples and cheese go well together, and cheese and apple pies are of some antiquity. Thinly slice 115g/4oz cheese (Cheddar, Lancashire, Wensleydale or even Stilton) and place on top of the apples before adding the pie top. Cream cheese works well, too. You can also add spices. An alternative is to replace about a third of the flour in the pastry with cheese, although it does make the pastry a little harder to work with. Or just eat the apple pie with cheese on the side.

• *Lemon and orange* ~ Add the grated zest of half a lemon or orange to the apple mixture, or a couple of tablespoons of orange marmalade.

• *Raisins* ~ Add 115g/4oz raisins or sultanas to the apple mixture.

• *Spices* ~ Add a teaspoon or so of spices, such as cinnamon, nutmeg or cloves – perhaps rather less of cloves – or a combination of them.

Cherry Pie

This should be enough for about eight people.

This recipe reminds me of a children's book called *The Great Pie Robbery* by Richard Scarry; the detectives found the canine culprits very easily, as their chops were smeared red from a delicious, stolen cherry pie.

For the pastry:
285g/10oz plain flour
140g/5oz butter, cold from the fridge
A few tbsp cold water
For the filling:
675g/1½lb cherries (fresh or tinned)

85g/3oz caster sugar
25g/1oz plain flour (optional)
45g/1½oz melted butter (optional)
To glaze (optional):
Milk or an egg white
25g/1oz caster sugar

1. Make the pastry (see p. 120). Roll it out into two pieces as explained on p. 146 and use the larger piece to line the base and sides of a pie dish.
2. Heat the oven to 400F/200C/gas mark 6 and put a baking sheet in the oven.
3. Remove the stones from the cherries. This is a bit of a bore if you do not have a cherry stoner (which fortunately will double as an olive stoner).
4. Mix the cherries with the sugar, and with the flour and melted butter if using.
5. Pour the cherry mixture into the pie dish.
6. Place the pastry lid on the pie and make a few knife cuts in the middle.

7. Brush the pastry with milk or egg white and sprinkle on some caster sugar.
8. Cook for about 45 minutes until the top is crisp and golden.
9. Allow to cool a little and serve with custard, cream or ice cream.

Variations
• *Alcohol* ~ Add 2 tsp Calvados or kirsch to the cherry mixture.

• *Almonds* ~ Add about 115g/4oz ground almonds to the cherries.

• *Almond extract* ~ Add a few drops to the mixture, but do stir in well.

• *Cinnamon* ~ Add 1 tsp cinnamon to the mixture.

• *Sugar* ~ Use brown or light muscovado sugar instead of caster.

Gooseberry Pie

Enough for about eight people.

For the pastry:
285g/10oz plain flour
140g/5oz butter, cold from the fridge
A few tbsp cold water

For the filling:
450–675g/1–1½lb gooseberries
3 tbsp caster or granulated sugar
2 tsp cornflour

1. Make the pastry (see p. 120). Roll it out into two pieces as explained on p. 146 and use the larger piece to line the base and sides of a pie dish.
2. Top and tail the gooseberries and put them in a saucepan with the sugar.
3. Dissolve the cornflour in a little water and add it to the saucepan.
4. Heat gently on the hob for about five minutes, stirring occasionally, before taking the pan off the heat. The fruit will turn a little yellow.
5. Heat the oven to 400F/200C/gas mark 6 and put a baking sheet in the oven.
6. Cool the fruit for about 10 minutes, pour it into the pie dish, cover with the pastry lid and cut a few holes in the top with a knife. Place on the baking sheet and cook for about 40 minutes.
7. Allow the pie to cool a little, and serve with cream, ice cream or custard.

Mince Pie

Makes one pie to feed about eight people.

Bought mincemeat often needs geeing up a bit, so try adding a few tablespoons of brandy (for some necessary alcohol), slightly less of lemon juice (for some bite), and about the same of almond pieces (to give it crunch). Mince pies and tarts (i.e. the little ones that you eat at Christmas) are greatly enhanced by brandy butter (see p. 79). If you are ur-man enough to make your own mincemeat, so much the better.

For the pastry:
285g/10oz plain flour
140g/5oz butter, cold from the fridge

A few tbsp cold water
For the filling:
450g/1lb mincemeat

1. Make the pastry (see p. 120). Roll it out into two pieces as explained on p. 146 and use the larger piece to line the base and sides of a pie dish.
2. Heat the oven to 400F/200C/gas mark 6 and put a baking sheet in the oven.
3. Tip the mincemeat into the pie dish, cover with the pastry lid and cut a few holes in the top with a knife. Cook on the baking sheet for about 40 minutes.
4. Allow to cool a little, and serve with cream, ice cream or custard.

Plum Pie

Serves eight.

For the pastry:
285g/10oz plain flour
140g/5oz butter, cold from the fridge
A few tbsp cold water
For the filling:
900g/2lb plums

115–140g/4–5oz sugar
To glaze (optional):
Milk or an egg white
25g/1oz caster sugar

1. Make the pastry (see p. 120). Roll it out into two pieces as explained on p. 146 and use the larger piece to line the base and sides of a pie dish.
2. Heat the oven to 400F/200C/gas mark 6 and put a baking sheet in the oven.

3. Remove the stones from the plums and cut up into quarters or smaller.
4. Mix the plums with the sugar, and add the mixture to the pie dish.
5. Cover with the pastry lid and cut a few holes in the top with a knife.
6. Brush the pastry with milk or egg white and sprinkle on some caster sugar.
7. Cook for about 45 minutes, until the top is crisp and golden.
8. Allow to cool a little and serve with cream, ice cream or custard.

Variations

• *Nuts* ~ Plums are good with almonds. Add about 60g/2oz ground almonds to the fruit, or try chopped walnuts.

• *Sugar* ~ Use white, light brown, demerara or even light muscovado sugar.

• *Spices* ~ A teaspoon or so of spices, such as cinnamon, is a good addition.

A few other suggestions for pies

You can try any fruit or combination of fruits, for instance strawberries or raspberries. If the fruit is likely to be particularly soggy when cooked, mix with some dissolved cornflour. Add any suitable spices. You can add some double cream and a couple of egg yolks to the filling, too.

• *Blackcurrant pie* ~ Try about 900g/2lb blackcurrants, or less if preferred, as the flavour is quite intense, but add a bit more sugar than for apples.

• *Blueberry pie* ~ As blueberries are quite a powerful taste, reduce the quantities to 450g/1lb or 675g/1½lb, but increase the sugar to about 140–200g/5–7oz to taste, and add a few tablespoons of flour to the mixture. Blueberries are nice with orange zest and juice.

• *Pear pie* ~ Use about 900g/2lb pears and 115g/4oz sugar. Cornflour (dissolved) will make the pears less runny when cooked. Do add some spices (cinnamon, nutmeg), and ground almonds or almond extract.

• *Rhubarb pie* ~ Use 900g/2lb of rhubarb and 115g/4oz sugar, with ginger or orange zest if wanted. A teaspoon or two of dissolved cornflour mixed in with the rhubarb makes it a little less liquid.

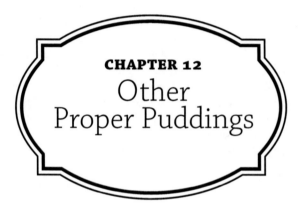

CHAPTER 12

Other
Proper Puddings

THIS CHAPTER is a ragbag of recipes that don't fit anywhere else. But they are too good to omit and so have been awarded a chapter all to themselves. The apple Charlotte is particularly good; and the chocolate microwave pudding is extremely quick.

Apple Charlotte

Will feed up to five or six ordinary people.

In one account, this pudding was invented by a famous French chef and named in honour of Queen Charlotte, the consort of George III. It consists of stale bread and butter, which surrounds an apple purée. Like summer pudding (and so far it is quite like summer pudding) this brief description might wrongly put you off one of the great desserts, which is also pretty simple to make. It is also a good use of old bread (and any old cooking apples) if you are bored of bread and butter pudding.

The one problem with apple Charlotte that I have encountered is structural failure: the pudding tends to collapse when removed from its bowl, another resemblance to summer pudding. As a result, I think it best to make the pudding rather small, and the ingredients below reflect this. I therefore often make two of these at the same time.

450g/1lb cooking apples
170g/6oz butter
1 tsp cinnamon or nutmeg or
  ½ tsp cloves (optional)

About 8 slices white bread
2 eggs or egg yolks
25–60g/1–2oz demerara, caster or
  light brown sugar

1. Peel and core the apples, and cut them reasonably thinly.
2. Put the apples in a saucepan with 25g/1oz of the butter, any spices, and a splodge of water to prevent them from catching. Cook very gently for about 20 minutes, stirring occasionally, until soft enough to whisk into a purée with a fork. Cool the apples.
3. Heat the oven to 400F/200C/gas mark 6.
4. Melt the remaining butter. It is easiest to do this by cutting it up into pieces and melting it in the microwave for 10 or 20 seconds at a time.
5. Remove the crusts from the bread. Soak each slice in the melted butter.

6. Arrange the bread around the sides and base of a basin so that the basin is entirely covered and there are no gaps. This may take a bit of rearranging and cutting of the bread. Keep back a couple of slices and some melted butter to make the top.
7. Beat the eggs or egg yolks and sugar into the apple purée.
8. Decant the puréed mixture into the lined basin. Soak the remaining bread in the butter and use them to seal the top of the pudding. If the bread slices protrude over the lip of the basin, trim them to fit.
9. Cook in the oven for about 30–45 minutes. The outside should be crisp and golden.
10. Eat with custard, cream, or crème fraîche.

Tips

• *Apples* ~ Cooking the apples takes at least 20 minutes or so, and you need to stir them occasionally. As the apples then have to cool, making an apple Charlotte does take some time, though you can speed the cooling to only about 10 minutes if you immerse the saucepan in a bowl of cold water after the apples are cooked (making sure none goes over the top).

• *Bread* ~ Thin bread is often recommended, but I think medium or thick slices are better. Mrs Beeton recommends the bread to be sliced half an inch thick, which is perhaps going too far.

• *Extra crunch* ~ Try sprinkling some demerara sugar into a buttered bowl before arranging the bread, and also sprinkle some on top of the pudding after it is assembled.

Variations

You can try pretty well any of the variations that you might have for apple crumble (see p. 47–8).

• *Apple and blackberry* ~ Replace about a third or so of the apples with blackberries, which should be mixed with the purée after it has cooled and the eggs have been added. Blackberry and apple is, of course, a classical mixture, and is very good in a Charlotte, but apples and many other fruits generally work well.

- *Apple and raspberry* ~ Replace about a quarter of the apples with raspberries, which should be added after the fruit has been cooled and the eggs and sugar added. I think this is tastier than just apples.

- *Apple and marmalade* ~ Use half a jar of marmalade, adding half to the apple mixture and pouring the rest over the pudding after melting with a tablespoon of water.

- *Breadcrumbs* ~ instead of bread slices. For 1lb/450g of apples, you will need about 350g/12oz of white breadcrumbs and 170g/6oz of butter. Make the apple purée mixture as described above. Melt the butter in a frying pan and fry the breadcrumbs until golden, which will take a couple of minutes or so. Then add the breadcrumbs and apple purée in layers, when they are both cool enough to handle. It is best to have a number of layers: breadcrumbs, apple, breadcrumbs, apple, breadcrumbs. Don't make each layer too thin. Cook for about 30–45 minutes at 400F/200C/gas mark 6. You can easily double the quantities if you want to.

- *Cinnamon* ~ Add a little cinnamon to the apple.

- *Dessert apples* ~ These will hold their shape in the pudding. Cut into slices and cook in a saucepan with the sugar, before cooling and putting into the bread mould.

- *Ginger* ~ Add 1 tbsp grated root ginger to the apple purée.

- *Lemon* ~ Add 1 tbsp lemon juice and the finely grated zest of about half a lemon to the apple purée mixture, and mix in well.

- *Other fruit* ~ Try, say, pears, plums, rhubarb or apricots (or about 60g/2oz of apricot jam stirred into the cooled apple mixture). You do not need to make a purée out of the fruit.

- *Sultanas and Calvados* ~ Nigella Lawson recommends adding sultanas soaked in Calvados into the apple purée, which is delicious. Try up to about 60g/2oz sultanas soaked in a couple of tablespoons of Calvados.

Clafoutis

Serves four people, or six at a pinch.

This pudding consists of fruit in a cooked, batter-like mixture. Surprisingly, for anything French, it is pretty easy to make, but then it is also a dish from Kent. I use traditional quantities rather than doubling them, because clafoutis is best if it is quite thin, with effectively one layer of fruit. You can, of course, double the quantities and use two dishes.

85g/3oz sugar
3 eggs
60g/2oz plain flour
425ml/15fl oz milk
425ml/15fl oz double cream

1 tsp vanilla extract
450g/1lb stoned black cherries
  (I normally use tinned ones, though
  fresh or bottled are better)

1. Heat the oven to 375F/190C/gas mark 5.
2. Beat together the sugar and eggs, add the flour, then the milk, cream and vanilla extract, and whisk them into a batter. Or just blend all the ingredients together in a food processor.
3. Put the cherries in a shallow but wide oven dish and pour in the batter.
4. Cook for about 40 minutes. The batter should be golden brown on the top, but custardy inside.
5. Eat hot, warm or cold, with cream.

Variations
• *Alcohol* ~ Add some suitable liqueur to the batter, such as eau de vie, brandy or kirsch.

• *Flour* ~ Try self-raising flour, or add some baking powder for a rather different effect.

• *Fruits* ~ Use other fruits, for instance apples, apricots (tinned or fresh), blueberries, figs, gooseberries, peaches (tinned or fresh), plums or prunes.

• *Spices* ~ Add half a teaspoon or less of spices, say cinnamon or nutmeg (particularly to apples).

Microwave Chocolate Pudding

There should be enough for up to six people.

This is a delicious pudding, which is very straightforward to make and takes only a few minutes to do. If there is any left, and there normally isn't, it keeps very well. It can easily be reheated in the microwave (and is much better warm than cold). The amount of flour does not sound a lot, but it really is enough.

225g/8oz good dark chocolate (yes
  really, I know it sounds a lot)
140g/5oz butter, cut up into half
  a dozen pieces
115g/4oz light brown sugar

45g/1½oz plain flour
½ tsp baking powder
3 eggs
125ml/4fl oz double cream
1 tsp vanilla extract

1. Melt the chocolate, then the butter, in the microwave. (Alternatively you can grind the chocolate to a powder in a Magimix, which is effective but incredibly noisy.)
2. Add all the other ingredients to the chocolate and butter and combine.
3. Transfer the mixture to a pudding basin and stretch clingfilm over the top.
4. Cook in the microwave on full power for seven minutes, then remove and leave for at least five minutes.
5. Remove the clingfilm, avoiding the escaping steam. Don't be tempted to turn the pudding out on to a plate, as it's quite gloopy. Serve from the bowl instead.
6. Eat on its own, or with cream.

Variations
• *Chocolate* ~ You can use milk chocolate, or a mixture of dark and milk, if serving to children.

• *Flour* ~ If you think this pudding is too gloopy for your taste, you can use a great deal more flour.

Sweet Potato Pudding

This should be enough for eight to 10 people.

I first came across this Jamaican pudding in *The Cook's Companion*, the standard Australian cookery book by Stephanie Alexander, while staying with friends in New Zealand. Since then I have found various recipes for it, and it is common in the southern USA as well. It is ridiculously easy to make. Despite its cosmopolitan origins, I think it must be the most controversial pudding I have made. Some people love it and ask for the recipe, others hate it, and I don't know why.

675g/1½lb sweet potatoes
25–60g/1–2oz butter
140g/5oz raisins or other dried fruit
140g/5oz light brown sugar
3 eggs
300ml/10fl oz coconut milk

1 tsp ground cinnamon
1–2 tsp ground ginger
½ tsp ground or grated nutmeg
1 tsp vanilla extract
1 glass rum or sherry (optional)

1. Peel the sweet potatoes and grate them. It is easiest to do this in a food processor.
2. Melt the butter, which is easiest in the microwave, 10 seconds at a time.
3. Combine all the ingredients in a mixing bowl.
4. Spoon the pudding into a buttered dish.
5. Bake for about one hour at 350F/180C/gas mark 4.
6. Eat with cream.

Variations
• *General* ~ Needless to say, the quantities can be easily varied. I like quite a lot of spices in this pudding, but they can be reduced. Some versions of the recipe greatly increase the amount of dried fruit or sugar, and some add a few ounces of plain flour, so do experiment.

• *Milk* ~ Instead of coconut milk, try milk, double cream or evaporated milk.

Om Ali

Sufficient for six to eight people.

I tried this first in Oman a few years ago, and was pleasantly surprised to find a sort of Middle Eastern (or more precisely Egyptian) bread and butter pudding. I have come across quite a few variations to this pudding since.

225g/8oz bought puff pastry
115g/4oz melted butter
115g/4oz dried fruit (raisins, sultanas, diced dried apricots, or a mixture)
225g/8oz chopped nuts (a mixture of any of almonds, hazelnuts, pine nuts, pecans, pistachios and walnuts)
2 tbsp flaked coconut (optional)

300ml/10fl oz double cream
900ml/1½ pints milk
85g/3oz caster sugar
1 tbsp rose water or 1 tsp vanilla extract (optional)
1–2 tsp cinnamon or nutmeg (optional)

1. Heat the oven to 350F/175C/gas mark 4.
2. Brush the pastry with butter and cook for about 15 minutes on baking sheets. The pastry should be crispy and coloured, and must be cooked in the middle. Remove from the oven and increase the heat to 425F/220C/gas mark 7.
3. Cool the pastry enough to be able to crush it into flakes.
4. In a large pie dish, alternate layers of crushed pastry with layers of the dried fruit, nuts and coconut.
5. Combine the milk, cream, sugar and rose water and heat to boiling point.
6. Pour the milk mixture over the pudding and sprinkle or grate any spices over the top.
7. Put in the oven and cook for 15 minutes. The pastry should absorb all the milk and cream, and the pudding should not be swimming in it. There is a slight tendency for the nuts to come to the surface.
8. Eat.

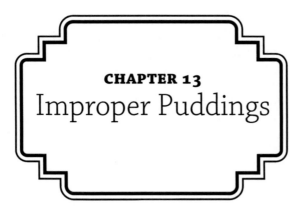

CHAPTER 13
Improper Puddings

THESE PUDDINGS, which might be better called desserts, are mostly for
the summer. I draw the line at so-called puddings that are basically just fruit,
whether raw, cooked or with cream, with the exception of fools and syllabubs.
As for fruit salad: ugh. Instead, these recipes are for things that don't meet my
definition of proper puddings, but which are still good to eat. Several of these
puddings are best made in small rather than large quantities (contrary to my
usual practice), and several need to be made immediately before eating (ditto).

Almond Pudding

This will feed about four people.

**This is effectively an almond tart without the tart, or Ipswich almond tart
without the breadcrumbs, and it is adapted from a recipe by Mrs Beeton.**

115g/4oz butter

225g/8oz ground almonds

½ tsp almond extract, or a few ground
 bitter almonds

4 eggs

Zest and juice of half a lemon

2 tbsp double cream

1 tbsp sweet sherry or brandy

1. Preheat the oven to 375F/190C/gas mark 5.
2. Melt the butter.
3. Add all the other ingredients to the butter and combine.
4. Put in a greased, ovenproof dish.
5. Cook for 45 minutes.
6. Eat, with some cream.

Variation
You can use up to 450ml/1 pint cream, provided you add 25g/1oz breadcrumbs.

Fools
Fools are ridiculously easy to make. The basic idea is to mix some whizzed-up
fruit with whipped cream, although Greek yogurt is a very good alternative.
Fools take very little time to prepare, but you need to start well in advance of
eating as the fruit normally has to cook and cool before you add the cream.

The name, by the way, comes from the French *fouler*, as the fruit is crushed, and does not refer to the fact that the dessert is so simple to make that even a fool could do it.

Rhubarb Fool

Will feed about four people.

I like to use ginger in this recipe, which is a natural partner for rhubarb, but you can add the zest of an orange instead.

450g/1lb rhubarb
About 85g/3oz sugar, to taste

1 tsp ginger (optional)
300ml/10fl oz double cream

1. Clean the rhubarb and chop it up in a food processor.
2. Put the rhubarb in a saucepan with the sugar and ginger and cook gently, stirring from time to time, for about 10 minutes.
3. Transfer the rhubarb mixture to a bowl and cool in the fridge for an hour or so. (You can cool it in half an hour if you put the saucepan in a bowl of cold water for a few minutes and then in the freezer.)
4. Whisk the cream until it is semi-solid, i.e. it makes little peaks. If it is too thick, you cannot easily fold the cream into the fruit.
5. Fold the cream into the rhubarb. If it is too gloopy, you can whisk again.
6. Eat.

Strawberry Fool

Enough for about four people.

Also known as pink stuff or stink puff. Unlike rhubarb fool, the strawberries do not need cooking first. This is, therefore, a pretty instant pudding.

450g/1lb strawberries
About 25–60g/1–2oz sugar, to taste

300ml/10fl oz double cream

1. Dehull the strawberries, a mild bore.
2. Whizz the strawberries up in a food processor, but not too violently or you get a liquid mush. It is likely that there will be some largeish bits left, but that's not a problem.
3. Transfer to a bowl and mix in the sugar.
4. Whisk the cream until it is semi-solid, i.e. it makes little peaks. If it is too thick, you cannot easily fold the cream into the fruit.
5. Fold the cream into the strawberries. If it is too gloopy, you can whisk again.
6. Eat.

Gooseberry Fool

Sufficient for four people.

This is very much like rhubarb fool in the making. It is deliciously tart, but not to the taste of most children.

450g/1lb gooseberries
25–60g/1–2oz butter (optional)

About 85g/3oz sugar, to taste
300ml/10fl oz double cream

1. Top and tail the gooseberries. This is the slightly boring part, and it does take five minutes or so.
2. Melt the butter in a pan, add the gooseberries and sugar to taste (or, if you prefer, add the sugar when they're cooked). You can use more sugar than is specified, if needed. Cook gently for about five or preferably 10 minutes, until they are soft and becoming pulpy.
3. Mash the gooseberries a little bit with a wooden spoon. Ideally you do not want complete mush, but you could (and I tend to) just purée the fruit instead.
4. Cool the fruit for an hour or so in the fridge. This can be done much quicker by immersing the pan in a large bowl of cold water for 10 minutes, which gets you most of the way.
5. Whisk the cream until it is semi-solid, i.e. it makes little peaks. If it is too thick, you cannot easily fold the cream into the fruit.
6. Fold the cream into the gooseberries. If it is too gloopy, you can whisk again.
7. Eat.

Some other fools

Here are just a few ideas. Try mixing up different fruits, for instance rhubarb and raspberry. For four people, use 450g/1lb fruit and 300ml/10fl oz of cream, which will serve about four people.

• *Apples* ~ Simmer 450g/1lb peeled, cored and sliced apples with 85g/3oz sugar and a few tablespoons of cider and Calvados for 10 minutes. Alternatively, try equal quantities of apple and blackberry with a little sugar: the apples will need simmering a little, and the fruit will need liquidising. Cool, then fold in the whisked cream.

• *Apricots, peaches or nectarines* ~ The fruit, tinned or better fresh, will need whizzing up. If you are fussy you could peel the fruit, but I don't bother.

• *Custard* ~ Try replacing half of the cream with custard, Greek yogurt, crème fraîche, fromage frais or sour cream.

• *Damsons* ~ Simmer 450g/1lb of damsons with 85g/3oz of sugar (perhaps brown) and a little water, for 10 minutes or so. Remove the stones, which is most easily done by pushing the cooked mixture through a sieve. Cool, and fold in the whisked cream.

• *Passion fruit* ~ These are great in a fool, preferably with a mixture of cream and Greek yogurt. You do not need to do anything to the fruit (other than cut it up and take out the edible middle): the pips can be left in and eaten.

• *Pineapple* ~ Whizz up the fruit (after peeling and coring) and fold into the whipped cream.

• *Plums* ~ Simmer the fruit with sugar, and then sieve or liquidise.

• *Raspberries* ~ They do not need cooking, only whizzing, perhaps with a little sugar.

• *Spices and alcohol* ~ Try adding some spices, or alcohol. For instance, try damson and whisky fool.

Fritters

This is enough for about four people.

Fritters are usually made from fruit that is coated in batter and then fried. The crisp outside contrasts with the softer fruit centre. They need to be eaten immediately, so they cannot be wholly prepared in advance, and the cook will normally be frying away while the other diners are eating the fritters. They require a little bit of technique and thus practice, but don't be put off: they are not difficult. They were part of my childhood, but I fear that they have rather died out, at least at home. They are particularly good for a family meal, as almost all adults and children like them.

450g/1lb fruit (see suggestions below)   About 2 tbsp milk
115g/4oz flour, plain or self-raising   Deep fat or oil for frying
A pinch of salt   Some sugar for sprinkling over the
2 eggs, beaten   fruit after cooking

1. Sift the flour and salt into a bowl.
2. Add the eggs and milk, and beat together with a wooden spoon or a whisk. The batter needs to be thick enough to coat the fruit, which requires a bit of judgement. It benefits from being left to stand a little.
3. Cut the fruit into pieces. Dry them a bit if needed, or the juices may dilute the batter coating.
4. Prepare the fruit by turning the pieces over in the batter with some tongs. It does not always cover all the fruit as it should, but that should not be too much of a problem. Let it drip a little.
5. Heat the oil or fat in a saucepan. I think sunflower oil is the most obvious choice. The oil must be about 2.5cm/1in deep, which will use about 600ml/ 1 pint oil, depending on the size of the pan.
6. Fry the fritters until crisp and golden, which takes only a few minutes. Cook only small amounts at a time, and turn the fruit over halfway through.
7. Remove the fruit from the oil with a little sieve, or with tongs. Serve immediately, as fritters need to be eaten hot. Serve sprinkled with sugar (ideally icing sugar, perhaps with spices added) and perhaps with a bit of cream.

Which fruit?
The following are the more common fruits used to make fritters. I tend to use a mixture all at the same time.

• *Apples* ~ Dessert apples are normally used, but cooking ones will do, too. Peel, core and thickly slice the apples. To avoid apple rings breaking up, core the apples before peeling. Or just cut into chunks. You can soak the apples for a few hours in 25g/1oz or so of icing sugar and a few tablespoons of brandy or rum. Apple fritters can be served with a sauce made from heated apricot jam and brandy (the brandy can come from earlier soaking).

• *Apricots* ~ Use halves of tinned or fresh (and peeled) apricots.

• *Bananas* ~ Peel and halve some ripe bananas, or use chunks of banana. Try soaking the bananas in a little rum first.

• *Oranges* ~ Peel the oranges and break them into pieces of one to three segments.

• *Peaches* ~ Use halves of peaches, either tinned or fresh (but peel them first).

• *Pears* ~ Peel, core and quarter some just-ripe pears.

• *Pineapples* ~ Use fresh or tinned rings. perhaps soaked in some brandy first.

And finally... Try figs, gooseberries, prunes, rhubarb (preferably young, and you will definitely need some sugar), strawberries (which go a bit soggy), bread, bread and butter or stale cake.

Cooking tip
The oil must be hot enough to seal the batter as soon as it is put in the saucepan. If it is too hot, the outside of the batter can burn before either the batter next to the fruit is cooked or the filling has had time to get hot. If the oil is too cool, the fritters takes longer to cook, and will be soggier. The batter takes a bit of time to heat and cool, if you get the temperature wrong. Some people use a thermometer to get the temperature just right. I hope these warnings do not put you off: it does not require too much judgement or experience to get it right.

Variations and additions

• *Alcohol* ~ Replace one of the tablespoons of milk with brandy, rum or sherry.

• *Almond extract* ~ Try adding a few drops in the batter for peaches or pears.

• *Butter* ~ Add 15g/½oz melted butter to the batter mixture.

• *Egg whites* ~ Whisk a couple of egg whites and fold them into the batter mixture last, after it has stood.

• *Juice* ~ If using tinned fruit, add a couple of tablespoons of the juice to the batter mixture.

• *Spices* ~ Add ½ tsp spices to the mixture, either mixed spice, or cinnamon (particularly good for apples) or cloves (ditto).

• *Sugar* ~ I have not suggested any sugar in the batter mixture. This may be a little unsugary for some tastes, depending on the fruit used. There are three methods: soak the fruit in an alcohol and sugar mixture beforehand for a couple of hours; toss the fruit in sugar (perhaps with spices) before dipping it in the batter; or sprinkle some sugar on after cooking, which I think is easiest.

• *Water* ~ Use water in the batter instead of milk.

Mousses

A mousse consists of whisked egg whites, which are folded into a flavoured base to make a cold dessert (see instructions on making soufflés for more detail). This can go wrong, but the process is much less critical than when used for hot soufflés. While the whipped ingredient is normally egg white, sometimes whipped cream is used instead, but I think this is rather too rich and heavy. The mousse will need to be chilled before eating for at least several hours, and it tends not to last for more than a day or so.

Gelatine can be added to a mousse to ensure that it retains its shape. Little packets of the stuff can be found in the baking sections of supermarkets. The granules need to be completely dissolved in a little water; just follow the simple instructions on the packet.

Chocolate Mousse

This quantity is sufficient for about three greedy children.

I will start with a chocolate mousse recipe largely borrowed from Nigella Lawson. It is much appreciated by small children (particularly if dark chocolate is not used), although adults like it, too.

115g/4oz good chocolate   1 tbsp water
1 tbsp golden syrup (or 1 tbsp caster   2–3 eggs
  sugar)

1. Break up the chocolate and melt it. This can either be done over a low heat, or in the microwave for 10 or 20 seconds at a time.
2. Separate the eggs.
3. Add the syrup, water and egg yolks to the chocolate, mixing the ingredients together.
4. Whisk the egg whites so that they form soft peaks. Fold them into the chocolate mixture.
5. Leave the mousse in the fridge for several hours before eating, preferably overnight.

Other chocolate mousses

Chocolate mousses come in many variations, following the idea of a base of melted chocolate, egg yolks and sugar, to which the whisked egg whites are added. You might, for instance, replace the water with the juice of about half an orange, some strong coffee, some Grand Marnier, brandy or Amaretto. You can use white chocolate instead of dark, and add some vanilla extract. Try adding 25g/1oz or so of butter to the base.

Fruit mousses

Fruit mousses use about twice as much fruit as chocolate, i.e. 225g/8oz or thereabouts. Soft ripe fruit such as peaches only need to be peeled, but firmer fruits need to be cooked first until soft. Cooked or otherwise, the fruit must be puréed before it is added to the mixture.

Pancakes

This basic recipe is supposed to be enough for six, but will, in fact, serve four.

I graduated to pancakes as a pudding from breakfast pancakes, which are demanded by my children pretty well every weekend. They need to be eaten instantly, or at least pretty soon after cooking.

For the pancakes:
225g/8oz plain flour
2 eggs
60g/2oz melted butter (optional)
60g/2oz sugar (optional)

600ml/1 pint milk
A pinch of salt
To serve:
Juice of a couple of lemons
Caster sugar

1. Make the batter for the pancakes a couple of hours before you want to cook and eat them; the starch granules need time to expand and absorb the milk. Just blend all the ingredients together in a food processor, or combine all the ingredients except for the milk, then add it gradually.
2. Prepare everything for frying the pancakes before cooking them: put the batter and a ladle next to the stove; have the oven on low with a plate in it for any pancakes that are not eaten instantly; and have serving plates, lemon and sugar ready.
3. Pour a thin layer of sunflower oil into a frying pan (or melt some butter in it) and heat until warm or hot. Add a few ladles of batter into the pan. I tend to make three or four smallish pancakes, and thus ladle in the batter in little circles not too close to each other. But you can of course make one big pancake, covering most of the frying pan.
4. Fry for a few minutes, then turn over with a spatula (I think it is not worth trying to flip them), and fry the other side.
5. Transfer to a warm plate and fold over. Serve soon and preferably immediately with some lemon and sugar.

Variations
• *Apple pancakes* ~ For the apple mixture, which should be prepared before you cook the pancakes, you will need about 900g/2lb cooking apples, 115g/4oz sugar, 60g/2oz butter, ½ tsp ground cinnamon, and 60g/2oz raisins. Peel, core and slice the apples, and cook gently in a saucepan with the butter and sugar

until the apples become a purée. This may take 20 minutes or so. Stir in the cinnamon and raisins. Spoon some of the mixture into each cooked pancake and roll up. Dust with icing sugar and serve.

• *Blueberries* ~ Add blueberries to the pancakes when they're almost set on top, a minute or two after adding the batter mixture to the frying pan. Good with maple syrup.

• *Cream cheese* ~ Mix 225g/8oz cream cheese with an egg yolk, 60g/2oz of sugar and some raisins. Put a spoonful of the mixture in each cooked pancake, fold it, and brown each one in the frying pan. Sprinkle with sugar and serve.

• *Other fruit* ~ Add any fruit mixture you like to the middle of the pancake. For instance, try 255g/8oz strawberries, perhaps with some fromage frais and a little sugar, warmed up if you like.

Crêpes Suzette

Serves four.

These are just pancakes with an orange sauce. For extra orange, try adding the zest of an orange to the batter. You can also stir some crème fraîche into the mixture before the pancakes are added.

Pancake batter (see above) – about half the quantity
60g/2oz butter
Grated zest and juice of 2 oranges

25g/1oz sugar (white, light brown or light muscovado)
3 tbsp Grand Marnier, Cointreau, brandy or a mixture

1. Melt the butter in a large frying pan, add the orange zest and juice and the sugar and heat gently.
2. Cook the crêpes in another frying pan. Fold each crêpe into quarters, and add to the first pan, coating them with the sauce.
3. Pour on the alcohol, and cook gently for a couple of minutes until slightly caramelised. (An alternative is to flame the alcohol and pour over the pancakes). Serve.

Pavlova

Serves four to six people.

This was invented down under when the Russian ballerina Anna Pavlova visited Australia and New Zealand in the 1920s. The meringue should be crisp on the outside and soft on the inside, which takes a bit of practice to do well. This pudding is a good way to use up leftover egg whites.

4 egg whites at room temperature
A pinch of salt (optional)
225g/8oz caster sugar
2 tsp cornflour (optional)
1 tsp white wine vinegar (optional)

1 tsp vanilla extract (optional)
10 passion fruits
300ml/10fl oz whisked double or
  whipping cream

1. Heat the oven to 350F/180C/gas mark 4.
2. Line a baking tray with baking parchment.
3. Whisk the egg whites (and salt if using) in a large clean and dry bowl until peaks form.
4. Fold in the sugar, a third or half at a time.
5. Fold in the cornflour, white wine vinegar and vanilla.
6. Transfer the mixture to the lined baking tray, flatten the top and smooth the sides.
7. Put in the oven, immediately reducing the temperature to 300F/150C/gas mark 2. Cook for one and a quarter hours. Turn off and leave to cool in the oven for at least an hour.
8. When cool, turn the Pavlova upside down onto a dish, and pile on the cream and fruit (on which see below).

Toppings and variations
• *Fruit* ~ In place of the passion fruit, you could use strawberries, raspberries, grapes, kiwis, nectarines, peaches, pineapples or whatever, about 115g/4oz–225g/8oz in each case. Any larger fruit will need to be cut up into chunks, and of course the skins need to be removed.

• *Alcohol* ~ Add a tablespoon or two of brandy, Marsala or sherry to the fruit filling.

• *Chocolate* ~ This can be added to a suitable fruit, such as raspberries, oranges or strawberries. Try a few tablespoons of cocoa powder in the meringue, and 115g/4oz plain chocolate, melted or grated, with the cream and fruit.

• *Orange or lemon zest* ~ Add this to the cream.

Soufflé

This is the Richard Strauss of puddings: difficult; flashy; immediately attractive, but ultimately insubstantial. Listen to *Der Rosenkavalier* while eating soufflé and you will get the idea. Many soufflé recipes are very complicated, but I have included only relatively straightforward ones. They do, though, require some technique and experience, unlike any proper pudding.

Soufflés have two parts: a base, which has the flavour, and some whisked egg whites, which are the raising agent. The two things that require practice to get right are whisking the egg whites to the right consistency, and folding the base and egg whites together so they are mixed enough without losing too many of the air bubbles from the egg whites.

Some helpful tips

• Have the oven heated in advance. The correct temperature is about 375–400F/ 190–200C/gas mark 5–6. Any hotter and the outside will be crusty and the inside uncooked. Reducing the heat to 350F/180C/gas mark 4 and lengthening the cooking time is fine, but no lower.
• The dish is important; it needs to be the right size, so that the mixture comes up to within about 1cm/½in of the top. A soufflé dish should have straight sides and be made of relatively thin china so that the heat penetrates quickly. You can also use individual soufflé dishes, in which case reduce the cooking time to 12–15 minutes.
• Prepare the dish in advance. Butter it well, so that the soufflé can rise without sticking to the sides. It also helps to sprinkle some sugar on the inside of the dish, which acts as ball bearings. Add a spoonful on one side, shake the dish around so that sugar sticks to the buttery sides, and then turn upside down to get rid of any excess. Some people put a paper collar around the dish to stop the soufflé falling over when it has risen, but I think that is unnecessary.
• Make the base first. It should not be too solid, nor too sloppy. Nor should it be too hot when the whisked egg whites are folded in; tepid or something near

room temperature is best. If you are adding flour to the base (25g/1oz plain flour), make a roux by cooking it gently with the melted butter on the stove.
• Make sure that the whites have no bits of yolk or shell in them, and that the bowl is clean and dry.
• Whisk the egg whites so that they stand in peaks. This process adds little air bubbles into the egg whites, and when cooking they expand, making the soufflé rise. It is important not to overbeat, because you lose bubbles and it will be harder to fold the egg whites into the base.
• Immediately fold the egg whites into the base, so the mixture is reasonably well mixed; the fact that there is some variation in texture does not really matter too much, though if not well mixed enough, the mixture may rise unevenly. What is to be avoided is losing too many of the air bubbles that have been beaten in. You can help this by:
  ~ Not beating the whites too stiff, because they will not fold in well.
  ~ Using a metal spoon for folding, rather than a wooden one.
  ~ Mixing a spoonful of the whites into the base first, then mixing in the rest.
  ~ A bit of practice.
• Immediately scrape the mixture into the soufflé dish with a spatula and transfer it to the oven. You can look at the soufflé while cooking, but it is best to leave it if you can.
• Do not overcook. It is sometimes said that a soufflé is cooked when a skewer comes out reasonably clean, but I tend to take it out before that. I have seen recipes that double the normal cooking time of 15–20 minutes, or even more. I think this is too much, though it is often recommended if you have added flour to the mixture (25g/1oz plain flour to the base). Individual soufflés will only need 12–15 minutes.
• You can dust with caster sugar when removed from the oven if you like. Or dust before the soufflé goes into the oven.
• Eat straight away, as the soufflé will start shrinking within a minute or two. The eaters should be ready, clutching their spoons.

A word on quantities
A four-egg soufflé is supposed to be enough for four people. I think it is a bit mean, and better for three. For four reasonably greedy adults, I increase the quantities by 50 per cent. If you are feeling brave, make two big soufflés for six to eight people, but I think this can only be an *amuse-bouche* before the pudding proper.

Chocolate Soufflé

Serves three or four.

This is perhaps the most popular soufflé, and it is relatively straightforward.

115g/4oz dark chocolate
About 1 tbsp water

60g/2oz caster sugar
4 eggs

1. Preheat the oven to 375–400F/190–200C/gas mark 5–6 and prepare the soufflé dish (see p. 173).
2. Separate the eggs.
3. Melt the chocolate. This can either be done on the stove on a gentle heat, or in the microwave for 10 or 20 seconds at a time until melted.
4. Add the sugar to the melted chocolate, and then the egg yolks, mixing thoroughly. If too stiff, you may need 1 tbsp or so of water (or use alcohol or orange juice – see variations below).
5. Whisk the egg whites, fold into the chocolate mixture, put in the soufflé dish, and transfer to the oven.
6. Cook for about 15–20 minutes.
7. Eat immediately, adding cream if wanted.

Variations

• *Alcohol* ~ Add 2–3 tbsp rum or brandy to the base.

• *Apple* ~ Cook two peeled, cored eating apples into a purée and add to the base.

• *Cocoa* ~ This is an alternative to chocolate, but it is not as good.

• *Coffee* ~ Try strong black coffee as a liquid to add to the base.

• *Milk chocolate* ~ I can't recommend this, but children may prefer it. However, I find that they don't generally like soufflé much.

• *Orange* ~ Use orange juice in place of the water, and include the grated zest.

• *Vanilla* ~ Add a teaspoon of vanilla extract to the base.

Lemon Soufflé

Sufficient for three or four.

The problem I tend to have with lemon soufflé is that it does not rise quite as well as some others, given the relatively large quantity of base. But with luck, one should still end up with a delicious frothy pudding, a bit like a superior lemon meringue pie without the tart base.

2 lemons	115g/4oz caster sugar
60g/2oz butter	4 eggs

1. Preheat the oven to 375–400F/190–200C/gas mark 5–6 and prepare the soufflé dish (see p. 173).
2. Zest and juice the lemons.
3. Melt the butter on a low heat in a large saucepan. Add the zest and juice and half the sugar, mix in, and bring to the boil.
4. Separate the eggs. Beat the egg yolks together and stir them into the lemon base mixture.
5. Whisk the egg whites, add the remaining sugar and beat a little more.
6. Fold the beaten egg whites into the lemon mixture, put in the soufflé dish, and transfer to the oven.
7. Cook for about 15–20 minutes.
8. Eat immediately, adding cream if wanted.

Raspberry Soufflé

Enough for three or four people.

The large quantity of raspberries doesn't seem to overwhelm the egg whites. There is, however, a tendency for some of the raspberry sludge to congregate in the bottom of the soufflé dish after cooking, but one can simply pour it over the top of the pudding when in the bowls. As soufflés go, this is a relatively healthy one, as egg yolks are not necessary. The recipe should work for other similar fruits, for instance loganberries or strawberries.

300g/11oz raspberries
85–115g/3–4oz caster sugar
1 tsp vanilla (optional)

An egg yolk (optional)
4–5 egg whites

1. Heat the oven to 375–400F/190–200C/gas mark 5–6 and prepare the soufflé dish (see p. 173).
2. Purée the raspberries with half of the sugar, and add the vanilla and the egg yolk.
3. Whisk the egg whites, add the remaining sugar and beat a little more.
4. Fold the beaten egg whites into the raspberry mixture, spoon into the soufflé dish and transfer to the oven.
5. Cook for about 15–20 minutes.
6. Eat immediately, adding cream if wanted.

Variations
A teaspoon of framboise or kirsch is a nice addition. Add it to the raspberry mixture before whisking the egg whites. Or try a little lemon juice.

Grand Marnier Soufflé

Serves four.

I have read literally dozens of recipes for this soufflé, as it is very popular. Here is my relatively simple version. Many others use a flour base. You can replace the Grand Marnier with other liqueurs. I have tried Amaretto, Benedictine and others with some success.

2 egg yolks
4–5 egg whites

100ml/3½ fl oz Grand Marnier
60g/2oz caster sugar

1. Preheat the oven to 375–400F/190–200C/gas mark 5–6 and prepare the soufflé dish (p. 173).
2. Beat the two egg yolks, add half of the sugar, and then add and mix in the Grand Marnier.
3. Whisk the egg whites, add the remaining caster sugar and beat them a little more.

4. Fold the beaten egg whites into the base, spoon into the soufflé dish, and transfer to the oven.
5. Cook for about 15–20 minutes.
6. Eat immediately, adding cream if wanted.

Summer Pudding

This will feed four big people or six small ones.

Summer pudding is a mixture of soft fruit and old bread. It sounds disgusting, but it's actually delicious. It is neither difficult nor particularly time-consuming to make. About the only two potential problems that can occur are not having the bread properly soaked in the fruit, and structural failure (see below), which can sometimes be a bit tricky to avoid. Summer pudding can be frozen. Note that all quantities are very approximate.

900g/2lb soft summer fruit, traditionally raspberries, redcurrants and blackcurrants, or redcurrants, white currants and blackcurrants

170g/6oz sugar
2–6 tbsp water
About 8 slices white bread, preferably a day old, with crusts removed

1. If the bread is too fresh, lay it out to dry a bit.
2. Wash the fruit and remove the stalks and leaves. If using strawberries (see variations below), cut them up into two or four pieces.
3. Put the fruit in a saucepan with the sugar and water, and cook in the order detailed in step 4. Be light on the sugar; you can add more to taste later.
4. Heat gently, stirring quite frequently to avoid parts of the fruits overcooking; if they do cook too much they tend to go mushy, which may contribute to structural failure. When properly hot, cook for a few minutes until the juices are running. Blackcurrants and redcurrants need cooking for several minutes, raspberries and blackberries need very little cooking, and strawberries none at all save for some heating up, so you may need to add the fruit in stages.
5. Taste to see if it is sweet enough, and if not, add a little more sugar or just make quite a tart summer pudding and add sugar when eating.
6. Cool the fruit. You can speed this up by dunking the saucepan in a half-full bowl of cold water.

7. While the fruit cools down, cover the inside of a pudding bowl with bread, cutting it to fit. Ideally, no parts of the basin should show through the bread. An 18cm/7in bowl (1.5 litre/2½ pint), is about the right size for this amount of fruit.
8. When the fruit has cooled a little, after 10 minutes or so, spoon it into the lined bowl, keeping back some of the liquid for later, say a cupful. It is easiest to drain some of the liquid from the saucepan first using a sieve.
9. Cover with the remaining slices of bread. I tend to put some of the reserved juice on top at this stage to ensure that all the bread will be properly soaked.
10. Place a small plate or saucer (plates are a better shape) on the top of the pudding, and anchor with some weights, for instance one or two full jam jars. The weighted plate should be pressing down on the pudding.
11. When cool, shove in the fridge. Put the pudding on top of a plate just in case juice overflows from the pudding.
12. Leave at least overnight. A day or two will not harm the pudding.
13. When ready to eat, ease out of the bowl. This should be done by gently sliding a palette knife between the pudding and the bowl. Sometimes you will need to go round a couple of times. Put a large plate over the top of the pudding, and then upend and remove the bowl. Easy? Not necessarily - see below on structural failure.
14. If, as often happens, the top of the pudding or some of the sides are not soaked through with the fruit liquid, leaving white patches, add some of the reserved liquid.
15. Eat cold with some cream.

Variations: what fruit?
You can make summer pudding with almost anything in season, for instance blackberries and apples, some rhubarb. Here are some of the combinations I have tried with some success.

• *Blackcurrants, redcurrants and raspberries* ~ This traditional classic summer pudding is along the lines of 225g/8oz each of blackcurrants and redcurrants and 450g/1lb raspberries. Personally, I find this a bit tart, and prefer other combinations.

• *Raspberries, blackberries and strawberries* ~ This combination has a mellower flavour than some other fruits. I use half of strawberries, and a quarter of each of the other fruits. Half blackberries and a quarter of the others, perhaps with some blueberries, works equally well. Some authors do not recommend strawberries, but I have used them with success. It is, though, important to cook them for a very short time only, as explained in step 4. These fruits will not all be in season at the same time, but they are relatively easy to get hold of. The out of season ones will be more expensive and will probably taste of less: I imagine they come from plastic tunnels in the south of Spain. With strawberries, I cut the end off to remove the green bit (which is easier than fiddly dehulling) and then cut them into two or four pieces, depending on the size of the berry.

• *Raspberries, blueberries and strawberries* ~ Blueberries are better and less tart than blackcurrants, and the mixture of raspberries and blueberries is a particularly good one.

• *Raspberries and redcurrants* ~ Use about four times the quantity of raspberries to redcurrants.

• *Strawberries, raspberries (or blueberries) and cherries* ~ Again, half strawberries and a quarter of the others.

Some tips to avoid structural failure

• Summer pudding can go slightly wrong by falling apart after it is decanted from the bowl. (But then it is a dessert, so what do you expect? Proper puddings can almost never go wrong.) This is not crucial; indeed you can simply serve the pudding from the bowl. However, if you want to try to avoid this, try the following:
• Do not overcook the fruit, or you end up with mush. Just a few minutes after the fruit has become properly hot is more than sufficient, less for strawberries.
• Get the right amount of juice in the pudding. Too much or too little is the main cause of structural failure, I think.
• Fill the pudding to the top of the bowl, if possible. If it is only two-thirds of the way up, the pudding will tend to fall apart when you take it out of the bowl.
• Use a palette knife to ease the pudding away from the sides of the bowl. This needs to be done gently, and sometimes a couple of times.
• The risk of structural failure is increased if the pudding is made bigger. Two smaller puddings are better than one large one.

Further tips

- *Choice of fruit* ~ It does reduce the effort if you use fruit that doesn't need de-stoning, which is always a bit of a bore. Blackberries and raspberries, for instance, are particularly good because they need virtually no attention before cooking; cherries are rather more hard work.

- *Custard* ~ Eat with cold custard rather than cream. For a custard fan, this is much recommended. Other alternatives are vanilla ice cream or crème fraîche.

- *Frozen fruit* ~ You can use frozen fruit. It is never quite as good, so it is best to mix frozen with fresh.

- *Trifle sponges* ~ Use trifle sponges split in half to line the bowl instead of bread.

- *Vanilla* ~ Add split vanilla pods or vanilla extract to the fruit before cooking, and/or the juice of half a lemon.

Syllabub

This improper pudding is ridiculously easy to make, but it is for grown-ups only. It's just double cream whisked pretty stiff, with some alcohol, sugar and perhaps a bit of flavouring, essentially a fool with some alcohol. Syllabub does not keep, and needs to be eaten in an hour or two, otherwise the mixture tends to separate. I sometimes make a syllabub in the summer when I am cooking an ordinary puddingless meal and find I have five or 10 minutes free while the main course is doing its stuff. The texture is nicely set off with some little hard biscuits, such as ratafias or whatever.

Lemon Syllabub

This is enough for three or four people.

If you think that this is too lemony, use just one lemon. An electric beater would be useful for this recipe, otherwise you will need to do an awful lot of beating with a hand whisk. You can double the quantities, or halve them for an ordinary meal for two.

1–2 lemons

120ml/4fl oz white wine or sherry, perhaps even some brandy

A little nutmeg (optional)

85g/3oz sugar

300ml/10fl oz double cream

1. Zest and squeeze the lemons.
2. Mix in the lemon zest and juice with the white wine or sherry and the nutmeg.
3. Stir in the sugar until dissolved.
4. Whisk the cream for a few minutes until it thickens, but not too much: if it is too solid, it is harder to combine the cream with the other ingredients.
5. Fold in the other ingredients. If it is too sloppy, whip a bit more; this works fine. (Alternatively, just add the unwhipped cream to the mixture and whip it all up together.)
6. Keep in the fridge until it is to be eaten.

Variations and other syllabubs

• *General* ~ The quantities given above are only approximate, and I have seen many recipes with quite varying proportions. Try replacing the cream with mascarpone, or the alcohol with pudding wine, Marsala or Madeira. You could also add a few well-whisked egg whites. There are, of course, many possible variations in the fruit and alcohol.

• *London syllabub* ~ No or little fruit is used, and the alcohol is normally Madeira.

• *Orange syllabub* ~ Replace the lemons with oranges and use a few tablespoons of Cointreau for the alcohol.

• *Passion fruit* ~ Try about eight passion fruits in place of lemons. Heat them gently, perhaps with some orange juice and sugar to make a pulp, and sieve to remove the seeds.

Trifle

There were some French Foreign Legionnaires marching through the desert, and they had run out of water. Suddenly they saw a marketplace, full of stalls. At the first stall, the soldiers asked for some water. The owner replied: 'I am afraid I have no water, only puddings made from sponge, fruit and custard.' Exactly the same thing happened at every other stall. As the thirsty soldiers marched away, one said to his mate: 'You know, that was a trifle bazaar.'

Trifles have a special place in my family due to my late maternal grandfather. He was a slightly eccentric man who lived to be 94, and who always had a cup of strong coffee and a hunk of cheese before going to bed, after which he slept like a log. Once, when he was a young man, he remarked that he could eat the whole of a large and delicious looking trifle, which had been produced by his hostess. On being challenged to do so, he obliged, with no ill effects – or so he said.

There are so many trifle recipes in ordinary standard cookery books that I don't feel the need to set out a great number. I think it is more important to describe the principles of a trifle, and then you can get on and make your own. Some you will read about can be pretty complicated to make. I am very fond of a very alcoholic one from Nigella Lawson's *How to Eat*, although I find it a bit fiddly. I tend to keep trifles simple, though the good thing about even a time-consuming trifle is that it can be made in stages, and well in advance. Indeed, trifles are probably best left for several hours, if not a whole day. Alcohol is a general problem with trifles: they are better with it in, but then they are not so good for children.

The idea of most trifles is to have three or four layers of cold pudding in a glass bowl. Perhaps they should each be described in turn. The precise quantities are rather unimportant.

The first layer traditionally consists of sponge cakes broken into pieces; you can buy them in a supermarket or make your own. Alternatively, and I think a little less satisfactorily, use trifle sponges, which you can get in packets in supermarkets, and which should be split in half. Spread raspberry jam on each piece. You can use other jams, depending on what will go with the fruit in the middle layer of the trifle. Sometimes, crushed macaroons or ratafias are added, too. You could use Swiss rolls instead. Soak the sponge cake in sherry, but you can use rum, or a mixture of the two, or Madeira, or Marsala and Grand Marnier, or whatever will fit in with the fruit used in the middle layer. Orange juice is the normal alcohol substitute: the sponge definitely needs moistening with something.

The second layer is normally fruit. The most traditional is probably raspberries, either fresh or frozen (and they do not need to be unfrozen). Any ripe summery fruit will do, for instance apricots, cherries, figs, kiwis (perhaps mixed with passion fruits), or strawberries. You could use even gooseberries or rhubarb (which will have to be cooked and sweetened first).

The third layer is traditionally custard. I think bought custard won't do, so make a custard as explained in Chapter 2. However, it will need to be set when cold, so use cream not milk, and probably just egg yolks (and quite a few of them). Cool the custard a little before pouring it over the trifle, and then chill the whole thing. You can flavour the custard, for instance with orange zest, alcohol or chocolate. As an alternative to custard – or an additional layer before the custard – use jelly. Or try mascarpone and dispense with the next layer of cream. The great advantage of doing this is that it removes the most fiddly and time-consuming bit of constructing a trifle, which is making a custard. Or, for grown-ups, use syllabub in place of the custard, and again you do not need a layer of cream on top. However, syllabub does start to separate an hour or so after making it.

For the fourth layer, spread over some whipped cream (either double or whipping cream). You can whisk some egg whites and fold these into the whipped cream. Decorate the top with flaked almonds, slices of fruit, glacé cherries or candied peel.

After this introduction, I doubt that any particular recipes need to be given, but I thought it might be helpful to offer a recipe for a pretty traditional trifle.

Traditional Trifle

- *First layer:* Break up half a dozen sponge cakes, spread them with raspberry jam, place them in the bottom of a decorative glass dish and soak them in 150ml/5fl oz sherry.

- *Second layer:* 225g/8oz raspberries.

- *Third layer:* Make 600ml/1 pint custard from 300ml/10fl oz double cream, 3–4 eggs, 25–60g/1–2oz caster sugar, and 1 tsp dissolved cornflour (see p. 24 for the method). Cool the custard before pouring it on the trifle, and then put the whole thing in the fridge for an hour or two.

- *Top layer:* Whip 300ml/10fl oz double cream, pour it over the trifle and decorate with some flaked almonds.

- Leave for several hours. Eat.

Zabaglione

Serves two to four people

Zabaglione (or *sabayon* in French) is easier to make than it looks, and it is pretty flash. The disadvantage, apart from requiring constant attention for about 10 minutes, is that, as with several of the desserts in this chapter, it is easiest to make in relatively small quantities and it is best eaten immediately, or it separates.

4 egg yolks   150ml/5fl oz Marsala
60g/2oz caster sugar

1. Put a large pan of water on to boil. This will heat the zabaglione, which is made in a bowl above it.
2. Mix the egg yolks and sugar in a bowl, and start to whisk them. Do not use too big a bowl, or it is harder to whisk.
3. Place the bowl containing the eggs and sugar above the pan of hot water and continue whisking until it is thick and pale and foams into a much larger volume. This is likely to take about 10 minutes or so, and is quite hard work and rather dull. An electric whisk is rather easier than a hand-held one; it is quicker but produces less volume than a balloon whisk.
4. Slowly add the Marsala while still whisking.
5. Spoon into some glasses and serve with crisp biscuits such as langues de chat or ratafias.

Variations
Try sweet white wine, sherry, vermouth, rum, Madeira, brandy or whatever instead of the Marsala, perhaps with a little lemon juice. This dessert is sometimes served with fresh summer fruit, or even bananas.

On Life, Death and Puddings

SYDNEY SMITH envisaged heaven as eating pâté de foie gras to the sound of trumpets. So far, so good, but what happens then? For me, the heavenly repast should end with steamed ginger and syrup sponge pudding with custard, eaten to the sound of flutes. (I am assuming that heaven is not too hot and thus a cold pudding appropriate, but I suppose that would be the other place.) I would like some roast grouse in between the outer courses, but that is another matter of no relevance to this book. Thus, before being transported to heaven or hell, and on the unlikely assumption that I both know the date of my death and still have a healthy appetite, I would know what my last meal should be. The pudding will, of course, be the most important part. I will then repeat Brillat-Savarin's last words: 'Bring on the pudding, I think I am about to die.'

People like and remember proper puddings because they are good, and surprisingly rare. But it is also of some importance that they are normally served as the last course, because we tend to remember the last part of any experience particularly well. Pudding should be served after cheese so that it is most memorable. It is wholly irrational that the British, who favour pudding over cheese, serve their cheese last. Our Hereditary Enemies, the French, adore cheese above almost anything and eat cheese before pudding, which is what we all should do. Puddings should always come last.

Acknowledgements

Thanks to all my friends and relations who have munched through innumerable puddings over the last 25 years, and especially during the last 10 while this book has been gestating. I would particularly like to thank Juliet Evans for her grammatical corrections; Nicholas Evans for inventing one of the puddings; my mother for her Christmas pudding recipe and for getting me started on puddings; Jonny Hughes for designing the book; Dilly Boase for the drawings; and most of all Joanna Swinnerton, who has edited the book and masterminded its production.

Further reading

I include this appendix just in case you have not had enough of puddings. I have found the following sources particularly helpful over the years.

General cookery books

The Book of Household Management, Isabella Beeton. The early editions are not that easy to follow for a modern audience. Later editions move a considerable way from the original, which is perhaps unsurprising given the passage of time. This is the *locus classicus* of traditional British food, and in particular puddings.

English Food, Jane Grigson. This has a very good chapter on puddings.

Complete Cookery Course, Delia Smith. This has good basic recipes for many types of pudding. For my taste, there tends not to be enough spice, dried fruit or cholesterol in her recipes.

How to Eat, Nigella Lawson (and indeed her other books). While there are not a huge number of puddings in her books, those that she has tend to be particularly good. I have been much influenced by her use of rhubarb and of Marsala.

Pudding books

There are several books on puddings that focus on light puddings or desserts. The following, though, mostly do the business for the real thing.

The Art of the Tart and *Tarts with Tops On*, Tamasin Day-Lewis. Some of the recipes tend to be a bit complicated for my liking, but they do work.

Good Old-fashioned Puddings, Sara Paston-Williams. This has a strong historical bent.

Real Fast Puddings, Nigel Slater. While mostly about light puddings, there are a large number of good ideas for the serious pudding person.

Great British Puddings, Mary and Debbie Smith. This is a good and well-structured book, although not particularly comprehensive.

The Classic 1000 Dessert Recipes, Carolyn Humphries. This is an extremely comprehensive book. The recipes are necessarily very short, and they tend not to be as rich as I would like them, but you can find almost everything here.

The Pudding Club Book, Keith and Jean Turner. This has nothing but proper puddings in, but the sheer number of recipes can be a bit overwhelming.

Internet sites

If you have a pudding in mind, a Google search is quite likely to give you quite a few recipes. The following sites are of particular interest.

www.cooks.com appears to have a relatively limited number of recipes under 'Desserts', but if you search for a particular type of pudding, you will find hundreds of recipes.

www.greatbritishkitchen.co.uk is a very useful site.

www.recipes4us.co.uk lists puddings under how long it will take to make them, which can be quite helpful.

www.uktvfood.co.uk has nearly 1000 recipes of all sorts under 'Desserts', mostly light puddings, but many proper ones too.